"Read this book and join the crusade!"

—Bob Hunter, President
National Insurance Consumer Organization;
Federal Insurance Administrator under Presidents Carter
and Ford

"Here is a simple, universal system of auto insurance that would cover us better and cost us less. I love this idea."

—Jane Bryant Quinn

"A crazy, radical, hare-brained scheme that is actually smart, conservative and practical. And fun reading!"

—Steve Brill, Editor-in-Chief
The American Lawyer

"This is a new-fangled version of an old-fashioned political pamphleteering screed of the sort that disreputables like Benjamin Franklin, Alexander Hamilton and Thomas Paine once wrote. Auto insurance is an outrage! How can we get some reforms like this adopted?"

—Peter Vanderwicken
Vanderwicken Financial Digest

"Tobias not only prescribes very good medicine for our sick auto insurance system; he also makes the medicine go down with clarity and wit. The next few years of our republic will test the power of sound ideas to prevail over special-interest fog machines. *Auto Insurance Alert!* revs the engines for just such a test."

—Michael Pertschuk, former chairman
U.S. Federal Trade Commission

"Pay-at-the-Pump is a unique, fair and practical idea. It eliminates the present bias against the young (a disproportionate percentage of whom are poor or minorities), eliminates insurance 'redlining,' and offers an affordable alternative to the millions of hardworking families threatened with criminal fines and jail solely because they cannot afford runaway insurance costs."

—Robert Gnaizda
Legal Counsel to the Mexican-American Political Association and 16 other minority and low-income groups seeking affordable insurance through litigation and legislative advocacy

AUTO INSURANCE ALERT!

ANDREW TOBIAS

A Fireside Book
Published by Simon & Schuster
New York   London   Toronto   Sydney   Tokyo   Singapore

FIRESIDE
Simon & Schuster Building
Rockefeller Center
1230 Avenue of the Americas
New York, New York 10020

Designed by Mary O'Neil
Manufactured in the United States of America

10 9 8 7 6 5 4 3 2 1

Library of Congress Cataloging in Publication Data is available.

ISBN: 0-671-79222-9

Contents

1. **THE DEAL IN A LUG NUT** 1
   (An Overview)

2. **CRAZY!** 15
   (An Analogy)

3. **PAY-AT-THE-PUMP** 17
   (No Salesmen)

4. **PRIVATE** 39
   (No Government)

5. **NO-FAULT** 51
   (No Lawyers)

6. **EMPOWERING THE CONSUMER** 63
   (The Report Card)

7. **COLLISION AND THEFT** 71
   (Yes and No)

8. **CONS** 83
   (The Arguments *Against* PPN)

9. **NEXT STEPS** 91
   (Making It Happen)

Appendix A: **What To Do In The Meantime** 95

Appendix B: **Safety Tips** 103

Appendix C: **Tear-Out Letters To Your Governor** 107

Author's Note

When *The Invisible Bankers* ("Everything the Insurance Industry Never Wanted You to Know") appeared in paperback, its cover blared: "The Shocking National Best-Seller!" The shock, of course, was that any book about insurance could become a national best-seller. Yet even then, in 1983, people were angry.

Ten years and about $1 trillion in auto insurance premiums later, things have only gotten worse. Auto insurance costs too much, it's too complicated, and if you ever do have a serious accident, it will likely fail to cover your costs.

There is a simple way to fix the system, and that's what this little book—which borrows from and builds upon portions of the last one—is about.

All royalties from the sale of this book will be donated to the National Insurance Consumer Organization, which promotes insurance reform, and to the Rocky Mountain Institute, which promotes energy conservation.

The woman cutting my hair at the Atlanta Airport, about 40 and articulate, narrows her eyes, leans close and whispers, with venom: "I'm paying $140—a month."

❏　　❏　　❏

In 16 years in Connecticut and Seattle, the marketing manager had received two parking tickets. Nothing else. No accidents. No claims. When she moved to Miami, she was told she was a high risk because she had no Florida driving history. The premium on her 6-cylinder Chrysler LeBaron convertible, with theft and collision coverage, but minimal ("10/20") liability: $1,800.

❏　　❏　　❏

"A drunk driver rear-ended me five years ago," writes a Tucson resident. "He injured me, and I am left with a disability and can no longer do what I was trained to do [dog grooming]. I have lost everything. My house has been taken over by H.U.D. I can no longer make my car payments and will probably lose it. I have had to go on food stamps.

"My son received a concussion and jaw injury. He was left with Petit Mal seizures. He had no problem like this before the accident. My daughter was left with four fractured front teeth and will need extensive dental work done when she's fifteen.

"I got a lawyer to take care of my case. Well, he really took care of it. He did not properly prepare for what the defense had planned. According to them, our injuries did not even exist.

"Anyhow, we were supposed to have been awarded $10,000. My lawyer called me and said could he sign my check since he had to pay the expert witnesses. I said yes under extreme duress. What he did not tell me was there was $1,500 left after his so-called expenses."

Chapter 1

THE DEAL IN A LUG NUT
(An Overview)

You could hardly design an auto insurance system worse than ours. With minor variations, it works the same in every state and it favors only three groups:

☐ Attorneys
☐ Insurance agents
☐ That small subset of accident victims lucky enough to be hit by someone heavily insured, where it can be proven that the heavily insured driver was at fault.

Under the current system, more than 40 cents of every auto insurance dollar is wasted. Nearly all that money could be saved.

And under the current system, the great majority of serious accident victims are tragically under-compensated. Only their lawyers do well.

What Auto Insurance Should Be

There's a way to fix this mess. And in many states it's now *such* a mess, and *so* expensive, that fixing it might actually be possible.

Granted, it will be tough. Few groups have a firmer stranglehold on our state legislatures than the lawyers and insurance agents who earn tens of billions from the status quo. They will fight like mad to preserve it—and they are, for the most part, very nice people. But there are a lot more of us than there are of them. Shouldn't auto insurance be designed to serve our needs rather than theirs?

The system that would do that is called PAY-AT-THE-PUMP, PRIVATE, NO-FAULT auto insurance (**PPN**). Here it is in a lug nut:

PAY-AT-THE-PUMP

Instead of buying auto insurance one policy at a time, everyone would be covered automatically. Most of the premium (not all)—very roughly 40 cents a gallon—would simply be added to the price of gas. We'd pay no more in auto insurance premiums than now (most people would pay less); but by paying at the pump, we would:

✓ Eliminate virtually all sales and underwriting costs. That would save about 15 cents of every premium dollar.

✓ Eliminate the "uninsured motorist" problem. (In some cities, nearly half the drivers are uninsured.)

✓ Eliminate the need to shop for auto insurance, fill out forms, puzzle over policies, pay bills, and carry proof-of-insurance cards.

The side-effects are equally exciting. By collecting the auto insurance premium at the pump instead of through the mail, we'd give people an incentive to drive more economically and use less gas. Which means:

✓ Less pollution
✓ Less traffic
✓ Fewer accidents
✓ Less dependence on foreign oil
✓ A lower trade deficit

Since we have to pay for auto insurance one way or another, why not do it in a way that minimizes costs and hassle; lessens traffic, pollution, accidents and our dependence on foreign oil; and eliminates the problem of uninsured motorists?

Although the bulk of the premium would be collected at the pump, there would be three other collection points:

❑ **Registration**—high-risk vehicles would pay a surcharge.

☐ **Licensing**—if we decide young drivers should pay more (but why? they'll get older—it all evens out in the end!), the computer could efficiently assess a surcharge.

☐ **Tickets**—on top of the current fines for moving violations, there would be a surcharge, because unsafe drivers should contribute more to the premium pool. (Right now, we "fine" many drivers in advance, whether they drive safely or not. Why not penalize only those who drive recklessly, and thus give them an added incentive not to?)

PRIVATE

Pay-at-the-Pump would be lunacy if the idea were to let the state government take over the insurance business. The last thing we need is another government bureaucracy. But that's not the idea at all. The state government would do just three things:

☐ It would collect the premium (efficiently, along with the gas tax it already collects).

☐ It would divide the state's registered vehicles into statistically homogeneous blocks of 2,500 or 5,000 (efficiently, by computer).

☐ It would invite all the auto insurers to bid for those blocks of business, much as private insurers now compete for group health insurance.*

But the government would not actually run the auction itself. Lest there be any fear of incompetence or corruption, the bidding process would be contracted out to a Big Six accounting firm, much as the Academy of Motion Picture Arts and Sciences contracts with Price Waterhouse for the Academy Awards (but with less tap dancing).

The rules of the annual bidding process would be designed to prevent abrupt or chaotic changes in market share. (For example, they might not allow any company to win an increase of more than50% in its existing market share the first year, no matter how attractive its bid.) But by and large, the privilege and profit of insuring blocks of drivers would go to the insurers who offered to do it at the lowest cost.

---

*Though there are a lot of problems with health insurance in America today, few would argue we should outlaw group health insurance. Yet for years that was exactly the case with auto insurance: under pressure from local insurance agents, the sale of group auto insurance was actually against the law in all 50 states! In many states, it still is.

When vehicle owners got their auto registration renewal, they would find the name and 800-number of the insurance company that had won their business printed right on it—efficiently, by computer.

If that company provided poor service in the event of a claim, drivers would do just what they used to do: complain. Only now the complaint would have more impact (see Chapter 6). And, just as now, in the case of true bad faith or negligence on the part of the insurer, abused insureds could sue.

NO-FAULT

But there would be a lot less suing going on, because we would stop spending billions of dollars fighting over claims. Instead, we'd spend those billions trying to make accident victims whole.

Drunk drivers would still be severely punished—maybe even more so than today. Reckless drivers would still face big fines. But if you were hurt in an accident, you wouldn't have to prove it was the other guy's fault; you wouldn't have to pray the other guy was rich (how many reckless teenagers carry million-dollar policies?)—and even if it *was* the other guy's fault, and you *could* prove it, and he *was* rich, you wouldn't have to wait years for your money and then split it with your attorney.

The main thing is to get the car fixed, not figure out who ran into whom. The main thing is to rush the accident victim to the hospital, chased by rehabilitation specialists, not lawyers, and to pay all his or her medical costs and lost wages.

We don't do that now for most serious accident victims; with a true no-fault system, we could.

I say "true no-fault" because the trial lawyers very cleverly gave us *fake* no-fault the last time this became a national issue. In all the states that purportedly now have no-fault, victims are free to sue for damages if their injury meets some—usually minimal—test of severity. So it's no-fault in name only.

As for pain and suffering, two things:

First, there could be a set schedule of payments for severe, incontestable injury—broken bones, disfigurement, paralysis and death, for example—that might peak at just $50,000 or $100,000. But at least it would be swift and sure and undiluted by legal fees.

Second—and this is very important—anyone who wanted to buy extra "pain and suffering insurance" privately would be free to do so. It wouldn't be a *good* buy, in all likelihood, any more than cancer insurance or flight insurance or most mail-order hospital and accident insurance is a good buy. But it should certainly be legal to sell it (with adequate disclosure), and people should certainly be free to buy.

How To Get A System Like This

So there it is—PPN: PAY-AT-THE-PUMP, PRIVATE, NO-FAULT auto insurance.

Of course, it's not this simple. Any thoughtful person will immediately have dozens of questions. What about electric cars? What about rural versus urban drivers? What about poor people who can't pay more for gas? What about driving across state lines?

But bear with me. *These questions have answers.* (You'll find a lot of them, in Q&A format, at the end of each chapter.) The folks who oppose reform have billions of reasons to keep you from thinking about those answers—namely, the billions of dollars that go into their pockets that, with PPN, could stay in ours. What they hope is that most people won't take the time to think this through. *Do you favor a gas tax?* they will ask incredulously, knowing that any red-blooded American will instantly shout, "No!" (But this isn't a gas tax.) *You want the government to settle your insurance claim?* they'll snicker. (But government wouldn't. The private sector would.) *If someone maims you, do you want to give up your right to sue?* (But what good is suing someone with only $100,000 of insurance—or none at all—when your medical bills and lost wages total five times that amount?)

The truth is, we need an efficient auto insurance system. Hard-pressed by global competition, America no longer has the luxury of wasting time and talent on things that don't need doing. To prosper, we can't keep buggy whip factories open just because nice people work there; we can't spend hundreds of millions of hours a year doing things—like selling auto insurance one policy at a time—that don't need doing. In the long run, we cannot prosper in the world economy by busily suing each other over claims. We have to *make* something.

We need nurses and math teachers, not people digging paper holes and then filling them back up.

It's not the *fault* of these people that they're doing something unnecessary. *They* didn't design the system! In fact, no one alive today designed it—it just "developed" in the days before computers . . . in the days before personal-injury lawyers advertising on TV . . . in the days before 200 million cars and trucks whizzing along at

high speed in the rain, in the dark, a few yards from one another
... in the days before medical costs soared. But times have
changed.

*So here's the plan: Read enough of this little book to decide whether
you think PPN makes sense. Then, if you decide it does, buy copies for
two or three friends and co-workers. When you do, two things will
happen. First, 100% of the royalty on the books you buy will go to the
National Insurance Consumer Organization, in Washington, which is
working to introduce PPN, and to the Rocky Mountain Institute in
Snowmass, Colorado, which is internationally known for its work
promoting sensible energy conservation. Second, and more important, the
word will spread. When enough people understand how simple and
beneficial a good auto insurance system could be—and why the lawyers
and insurance agents are so dead set against it—the system will finally
change.*

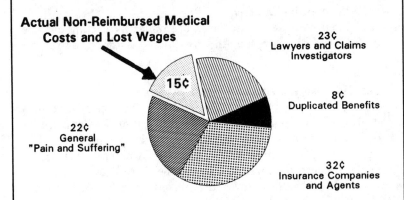

THE AUTO LIABILITY PREMIUM DOLLAR – *TODAY*

Actual Non-Reimbursed Medical Costs and Lost Wages

15¢

23¢
Lawyers and Claims Investigators

8¢
Duplicated Benefits

22¢
General "Pain and Suffering"

32¢
Insurance Companies and Agents

More than half our auto insurance premiums (and the interest insurance companies earn on those premiums) goes for "liability" insurance. Here's a rough estimate of where that money goes. Wouldn't it be nice if more than 15 or 20 cents of each dollar went where it was really needed?

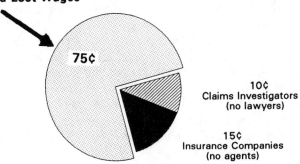

HOW IT WOULD LOOK UNDER *PPN*

Actual Non-Reimbursed Medical Costs and Lost Wages

75¢

10¢
Claims Investigators (no lawyers)

15¢
Insurance Companies (no agents)

Without lawyers and agents ... without having to pay duplicate reimbursements ... and without the fraud and inflated claims that the current "pain and suffering" formulae encourage, far more of the auto liability premium dollar would go where it's really needed: to reimburse people for their medical costs and lost wages.

QUESTIONS

1. What's the overall idea here?

To save 50 cents of every auto insurance dollar by cutting out the selling costs and the lawyers. And by cutting back on waste and fraud.

2. Whoa! How can you eliminate the sales costs?

By covering everyone automatically. Just add the cost of insurance to the price of gas (and to license and registration fees and traffic tickets, in order to make some adjustments to keep things fair). The more you drive, the more you'd pay for insurance. But that's reasonable, because the more you drive, the more likely you are to be involved in an accident (even if it wasn't your fault). For more on the issue of "fairness," see Chapter 3.

3. How do you eliminate the lawyers?

By having true no-fault auto insurance. Sure, a reckless or drunk driver could still be severely fined or sent to jail. And you could still sue General Motors if your car was defective, or your insurance company if it acted in bad faith. But you wouldn't have drivers suing other drivers. You wouldn't have to prove the other driver was at fault. (After all, often an accident is just that: an accident!)

4. How do you reduce waste and fraud?

By eliminating duplicate payments, and sharply restricting payments for "pain and suffering."

If someone has $9,000 in medical bills as the result of an accident, of which $8,000 are reimbursed by insurance, his net loss is $1,000. Under the current system, auto insurance pays the full $9,000 all over again—so the costs are reimbursed twice. And then, typically, the costs are tripled again, for "pain and suffering"—which may be real, but which also gives the injured party and his lawyer tremendous incentive to inflate those medical costs in the first place.

By cutting out nonessential coverages (is it really necessary to reimburse someone double for his hospital bill? can we afford that?), you greatly reduce the cost of the essential coverage everyone needs—and at the same time greatly reduce the opportunities for inflated claims and fraud. Separately, insurers could offer "pain and suffering" policies to those with money left over to buy more insurance. But a lot of people would rather spend or invest their money elsewhere.

5. Would all the savings go to me?

No. Much of the savings would go to accident victims. Under the current system, those who are badly injured don't get nearly enough to pay for their medical expenses and lost wages. Only their lawyers make out well.

You may say: "What do I care about serious-accident victims? I'm not one of them." But you could be. Or someone you love. Each year, more than 40,000 of us die in auto accidents and hundreds of thousands more are badly injured. In fact, isn't the *whole point* of buying auto insurance to protect against the possibility of a serious accident?

6. What other advantages would there be?

Well, there'd be no more uninsured drivers for you to subsidize. You'd be able to pay your insurance premiums in small, affordable chunks. You'd save having to shop for insurance, fill out applications, and pay bills. If you or a loved one ever *were* in a serious accident, you'd stand a much better chance of getting prompt reimbursement for your medical costs and lost wages. And Pay-at-the-Pump would be a boon to the environment.

7. How would it help the environment?

Collecting premiums at the pump instead of through the mail wouldn't cost the average driver a penny more. (Quite the contrary: being more efficient, it would save money.) But by blending the cost of insurance into the cost of gas, and thus raising the cost of gas, you'd give people an incentive to use less of it. That means less pollution, less traffic, less dependence on foreign oil—even a lower balance of trade deficit!

(Not to mention the trees you wouldn't have to chop to make the paper for 200-million insurance policies and applications and bills you wouldn't have to print and then add to the national trash heap—a very small consideration, but still.)

8. How would people conserve gas?

In the short run, there would be a little less driving, a little more carpooling, a little less traffic to get stuck in, a little more attention to tune-ups—all that. We're not talking about massive change or inconvenience, just marginal changes. On the margin, a few more of the people going from New York to Boston might decide to take the train, or fly. (Either is safer than driving, either saves fuel, and the plane is certainly faster.) Families with two cars might "take the small one" more often. Families with a bunch of chores to do might organize their routes a little more efficiently, driving down to the store a little less often.

Over the long run, there'd be more of a shift to fuel-efficient vehicles and to working closer to home.

9. How much would actually be saved?

One economist predicts that—in California alone—pay-at-the-pump would save 900 million gallons of gas a year initially, and 3 billion gallons a year once the effects of the higher gas price had had time to take hold.

10. But can people really afford such expensive gas?

More than they can afford auto insurance the way it's collected today! **For most people, the annual cost of driving would go _down_.** If we're going to collect a fortune in auto insurance premiums, anyway—and we are (in 1992: about $100 billion)—we may as well collect it in a way that cuts costs and helps the environment.

11. Who would be covered?

Everybody.

12. What kind of coverage would I get?

Far more than most people have now. Exactly what the benefits were—and thus the cost of the plan—would be determined by each state that adopted such a plan. But here is the model we have in mind:

- ✓ Total liability coverage (because under true no-fault, you'd _have_ no liability—you could not be sued).
- ✓ Total coverage for all your nonreimbursed medical expenses. (To encourage people to care about medical costs, there might be a small deductible: $100, or 10% of the first $5,000 in costs, whichever is greater).
- ✓ Total coverage for all your nonreimbursed lost wages after the first week, up to $25,000 a year (or, at your option, $50,000 or $75,000). In the case of a nonworking spouse, "lost wages"

would be based on the cost of performing household tasks someone else would have to be hired to do. In case of death, lost-wage payments would go to one's heirs, but cease after five years, or some similarly substantial but fixed length of time. (Auto insurance shouldn't be a substitute for—nor provide large duplicate payments on top of—adequate life insurance.)

✓ A modest schedule of benefits for "pain and suffering" in cases of severe injury.

✓ No-frills collision coverage (see Chapter 7).

Of course, anyone who wanted even more coverage would be free to buy it.

13. You're making the *government* my insurer?
No! Claims would be handled by private insurers, just as now—only better (see #16 and #17). PAY-AT-THE-PUMP NO-FAULT would require *no* new government employees.

14. So who'd be my insurer?
Whichever company won the right to handle your claims. It would be just like group health insurance or group life insurance—except that the group you belonged to wouldn't depend on where you worked, and you wouldn't lose your coverage if you lost your job.

Instead, the computer that spits out auto registrations would randomly divide vehicles into "groups" of 2,500 or 5,000. Private insurers would then bid for the right to insure those groups, just as they now bid for the right to handle an employer's group health insurance plan. State Farm might win the right to service 83 of the groups, Allstate might wind up servicing 61 of them—and so on.

15. Why would this be simpler for me?
Unless you had an accident, there'd be absolutely nothing for you to do. No shopping for insurance or filling out forms. No insurance policies to decipher. No bills to pay, no proof-of-insurance cards to carry around, no need to obtain insurance before driving off in your new car—none of that.

16. How would I file a claim?
The computer that spits out your auto registration would print one extra line at the bottom. It would read: TO FILE AN INSURANCE CLAIM,

CALL 800-NUMBER (namely, the number of the insurer to which your vehicle had been assigned). Whichever company had won the right to serve your group would answer the phone, just as it does now, and set about handling your claim, just as it does now.

17. But what if they don't treat me well?

Right now, all you can do if you're not happy with a claim settlement is complain. And you could still do that. (In truly egregious cases, you could sue your insurer, just as you can now.) But under Pay-at-the-Pump, Private, No-fault, your complaint carries a lot more weight. Every claim would be accompanied by a Claim Satisfaction Ballot (see Chapter 6). Insurers who got above-average marks from their claimants would be allowed to bid on more business the following year. Those who got below average marks would be cut back. Instead of simply *advertising* great service to win new customers, they'd actually have to *provide* it.

PPN's Customer Satisfaction Ballot would give insurers an extra incentive to settle your claim fairly and promptly. Right now, if an insurer treats you poorly it stands to lose only *your* business. Under the new system, it would risk losing *lots* of business. The fact is, most insurers already do a pretty good job of settling claims (especially no-fault claims made by their own customers). But under Pay-at-the-pump, Private, No-fault, they'd have an incentive to do even better.

18. What if I'm right in the middle of settling a claim when a different insurer wins the bid to service my business?

In bidding on blocks of vehicles to insure for a year, insurers would be bidding on the right to handle all claims arising out of accidents that occurred during that year. So if your accident occurred on the last day your vehicle was insured by Allstate, Allstate would have the obligation to see that claim all the way through, even if it wound up paying you benefits for many years. That's basically the way it works now, too: even if you drop an insurer or it drops you, any claims already in progress remain its responsibility.

19. I'm from Wyoming. You expect me to pay an extra 40 cents a gallon for gas?

No. A lower fee per gallon would be required in states where people drive great distances, because there would be more gallons over which to spread the cost.

And realistically, the need for PPN is certainly less pressing in a state like Wyoming than in California. Wyoming might be one of the last states to adopt a plan like this.

But even for Wyoming it makes sense. That's because whatever a state's drivers pay now for auto insurance, a huge portion of it is going for sales costs, lawyers, overhead, duplicated benefits and fraud—all of which PPN would greatly reduce.

20. I'm from Massachusetts. What's to keep me from driving to Connecticut or New Hampshire to buy my gas?

Nothing, which is why the first states to enact PPN would probably be those like Hawaii, or even California or Florida, where most of the population lives far from a neighboring state.

Soon though, seeing the benefits of PPN and wanting to secure them for their own citizens, groups of contiguous states might coordinate the introduction of PPN so that gas prices wouldn't vary much across state lines. (For more on cross-border problems, see Chapter 3.)

21. I can see why a guy who pays $900 a year for insurance might like this plan, but I pay only $200. Why should I be for it?

There will certainly be some who'll pay more under PPN than under the current system—namely, people who use tons of gas, yet enjoy low insurance premiums. And most of them will doubtless oppose this plan. But even for them there are benefits. The biggest is coverage. Does that $200 they now pay provide them unlimited medical benefits? And long-term disability if they're hurt? Surely not. How well protected are they against $1 million in medical bills or a $5 million lawsuit? It all sounds academic, I know—no one *expects* to be in a bad accident, or to have a child or parent or close friend involved in one. But as hundreds of thousands of people discover each year, it's *not* academic.

On top of that, PPN would make the economy a little more efficient, and thus a little more prosperous. It would treat car-crash victims more humanely. It would have positive environmental impacts. All that's worth a few bucks.

And there's this: Mightn't the low premium you pay today jump if you were involved in an accident? Or if you relocated to a higher-cost area? Or if you found yourself footing the bill for your kids' insurance for a few years? Viewed over a lifetime, and across an entire family, most people would come out ahead with PPN, even though some in any given year might not.

22. OK, OK—but isn't all this a pipe dream? How could we possibly switch to a system like this without creating havoc?
We would phase it in. Nothing would happen overnight. (See Chapter 9.) But it could definitely be done.

23. What happens if they enact Universal Health Insurance?
The cost of Pay-at-the-Pump, Private, No-Fault would go way down.

24. I still have a ton of questions.
Fair enough. This is only Chapter 1.

THE WHAT'S-IN-IT-FOR-ME WORKSHEET

	NOW	UNDER PPN
Cost of auto insurance:	Your current annual premiums:	Estimate from table on page 19:
	$_____	$_____
Maximum medical protection if you were badly hurt in a crash:	$_____	Unlimited
Maximum lost wage reimbursements:	$_____	Up to $75,000/year (see page 10)
Maximum protection if you injure someone who wants to sue you for $25 million	$_____	Complete Protection: you cannot be sued

How to use this worksheet: First, fill in the cost of your insurance now, versus an approximation of what it would cost under PPN (see page 19). Then imagine you were in a bad crash. How well would your current coverage protect you? Say you had $400,000 in medical bills. Say someone in the crash were permanently disabled. Say you were sued and a jury found against you in the amount of $3 million. It's these big, horrible possibilities auto insurance is really for. How well are you covered?

Chapter 2

CRAZY!
(An Analogy)

Forget automobile insurance for a minute. Consider unemployment insurance.

What if, instead of covering everyone automatically, as now, we required each employee to go out and buy it individually before he or she could take a job (just as we now require auto insurance before being allowed to drive)?

Group plans would be outlawed. A hundred million people would have to go shopping for a hundred million separate (though largely identical) policies.

Prices would vary widely, because—to be fair—the rate you paid would depend on the risk you posed. Among the factors that would go into determining your premium would be your seniority, the financial strength of your employer, the prospects for your industry, the transportability of your skills, the unemployment rate in your community, your history of prior claims, and so on. Young workers would have to pay more, because the most recently hired are the most likely to be laid off. Employees of start-up companies would pay heavily, because so many new ventures fail.

Insurance companies and local agents would advertise, help you fill out your application, collect your premiums, deliver a nice printed policy (with little onion-skin endorsements stapled to it), and provide you with a proof-of-insurance card to carry whenever you were at work. The penalty for forgetting to carry the card would be a fine, but the penalty for failing to have insurance at all would be severe. Your license to work could be suspended. Repeat offenders might even go to jail. The court system would be expanded to handle the load.

Finally, if you lost your job, and could prove your employer was at fault—that you hadn't just quit, or been fired for cause—40% of your weekly unemployment check would go to your lawyer for his time and expenses.

This plan would provide tremendous employment for insurance agents, clerical help, underwriters, advertising managers, lawyers and judges . . . but I think you will agree that it is unquestionably the dumbest insurance system anyone could possibly devise.

No one in his right mind would defend such a system!

And yet, of course, it is almost precisely the system we have now for auto insurance.

Chapter 3

PAY-AT-THE-PUMP
(No Salesmen)

In 1992, American drivers paid a bit more than $100 billion for auto insurance. If you were to spread that $100 billion over all the gas and diesel fuel we consumed that year—140 billion gallons—it would come to about 70 cents of insurance for each gallon of gas. But it's worse than that, because the 140 billion gallons of fuel we used includes fuel consumed by millions of vehicles being driven without insurance. (In some counties, close to half the vehicles are uninsured; nationwide, estimates are about 20%.) So if you spread the $100 billion over only the fuel consumed by *insured* vehicles, it works out that **you and I are now paying the equivalent of around 80 or 85 cents** in insurance premiums for each gallon of fuel we consume.

That's what we're paying now.

Of course, some people pay much less and some, much more. (And nobody pays for it by the gallon.) You can figure out your own numbers just by dividing your annual car insurance by the approximate number of gallons of gas you buy.

What You Pay Now

Say you pay $300 semi-annually to insure your car or cars—$600 a year—and that you drive 15,000 miles a year, averaging 15 miles to the gallon. You thus burn 1,000 gallons of gas each year. A $600 insurance bill spread over 1,000 gallons of gas works out to a cost per gallon of 60 cents.

If everything else in this example were the same except your car averaged 25 miles to the gallon instead of 15, then you'd use only about 600 gallons of gas a year—which means you're currently paying about $1 in insurance premiums for each gallon's worth of driving you do.

What You'd Pay Under PPN

The first question anyone is going to have (never mind the 24 questions at the end of Chapter 1) is: how would *I* make out under PPN? Is it going to cost me more or less?

And the answer for most people is: less. That's because there are no sales costs, no lawyers, no duplicated benefits, less fraud. And also because you would no longer have to subsidize those who drive uninsured.

But, as argued in Chapter 1 (Question #21), even if you figure PPN would cost a little more than you're paying now—because you consume far more gas than most people in your state, yet pay less for insurance—PPN may be in your interest.

Miles/Gallon I Get	GALLONS OF GAS I CONSUME ANNUALLY					
10	500	1,000	1,500	2,000	2,500	5,000
15	333	667	1,000	1,333	1,667	3,333
20	250	500	750	1,000	1,250	2,500
25	200	400	600	800	1,000	2,000
30	167	333	500	667	834	1,667
35	143	286	429	572	715	1,429
	5,000	10,000	15,000	20,000	25,000	50,000

MILES I DRIVE EACH YEAR

Miles/ Gallon I Get	WHAT PPN WOULD COST ME at 40 cents a gallon					
10	$200	$400	$600	$800	$1,000	$2,000
15	$133	$267	$400	$533	$667	$1,333
20	$100	$200	$300	$400	$500	$1,000
25	$80	$160	$240	$320	$400	$800
30	$67	$133	$200	$267	$333	$667
35	$57	$114	$171	$228	$285	$570
	5,000	10,000	15,000	20,000	25,000	50,000
	MILES I DRIVE EACH YEAR					

The table above shows *roughly* what you'd pay for auto insurance under PPN, depending on how much driving you do and the kind of mileage you get. (In states like Minnesota, with unusually low accident rates, the cost would be significantly less.)

You'd also pay something on the order of 1% of the value of your car at registration—about $100 on a car with a Blue Book value of $10,000. (See Chapter 7.) And you'd pay additional fees if you got ticketed for unsafe driving; and at registration, if you drive a high-risk vehicle.

As you can see, someone who drives 50,000 miles a year at 10 miles to the gallon would pay a lot for insurance! But this is not necessarily bad. Statistics show that the more you drive, the more likely you are to be involved in an accident, even if it's not your fault. On top of that, someone who commutes 100 miles each way to work—50,000 miles a year—and who drives a car that gets only 10 miles to the gallon (a limo? a hearse?) is spewing a huge amount of pollution into the air. If the added cost of PPN encouraged him to drive a car that got better gas mileage, take the train, or move closer to work, it would not be an entirely bad thing. In the rest of the industrialized world, gas costs about triple what it does in the US.

WHAT A GALLON OF GAS COST IN 1992

Britain	$3.69
France	$3.85
Germany	$3.85
Italy	$5.00
Japan	$3.75
Spain	$3.75
United States	**$1.19**

Source: International Energy Agency—*The Wall Street Journal*, June 9, 1992.

The Logic Of It

Why do we sell insurance one policy at a time that we require everyone, by law, to have? Imagine the added cost if we required everyone to contribute to the defense budget—as in effect we do—but then created a special sales force to sign them up one at a time. Or if we had to sell Social Security insurance that way. Or if we outlawed the sale of group health insurance.

Nearly 20 cents of each auto insurance dollar is spent signing people up. Much of that goes directly in sales commissions. But there's also advertising, sales management at the home office, the cost of sending bills and processing payments, and a whole slew of underwriters and actuaries who decide which vehicles to insure, which to reject, and what to charge.

Pay-at-the-Pump would save all that. And it saves *us* the trouble of *dealing* with it. No one ever puts a price tag on *our* time. But if the average driver spends just an hour a year worrying about auto insurance and paying the bills, that's 100 million person-hours each year—wasted. Wouldn't it be nice if life were a little simpler?

ANNUAL PAPERWORK REQUIRED		
	NOW	UNDER PPN
Insurance Applications	Tens of Millions	None
Insurance Policies	A Hundred Million	None
Bills Mailed Out	Hundreds of Millions	None
Payments Mailed In	Hundreds of Millions	None
Overdue Notices	Millions	None
Cancellation Notices	Millions	None
Reinstatement Notices	Millions	None
Proof-of-Insurance Cards	Hundreds of Millions	None

Think of insurance as a straight line with a point someplace in the middle. Up to that point, the insurer is working to get your business and collect your premiums. Beyond that point, it is working to settle your claims. For that's really about all automobile insurers do: they take in premiums and pay out claims. True no-fault insurance would greatly streamline the second function, the settlement of claims (see Chapter 5). But even more of their effort, and your dollars, are spent in the first: getting your business and collecting your premiums. To do this, hundreds of thousands of people are employed. They sell insurance, assign premium rates, examine applications, send out policies, send out bills, process payments, send out past due notices, send out cancellation notices. It is all unnecessary.

Uninsured Motorists

Pay-at-the-Pump would also end the problem of people driving uninsured, and the problem of trying to catch and punish them. Many of those people want to be law-abiding; they are just put in an impossible situation: there's no way they can afford $1,200 for auto insurance, yet they have to drive in order to get to work, and work in order to feed their families. PPN solves the problem by lowering costs dramatically and collecting the premium in small, affordable chunks.

Fairness

Perhaps the most obvious objection to paying at the pump is fairness; and you can be certain that this is an issue on which opponents of PPN will try to divide and conquer. They will ask older people if they really want to subsidize young, riskier drivers. They will ask rural drivers if they really want to subsidize city folk.

But there are two flaws in their argument. First, the savings PPN provides are so great that the cost of auto insurance will drop for almost everyone. That should make it attractive, even though some will benefit more than others. Second, there are simple, efficient ways to build fairness into the system. It will never be perfectly fair, of course. But how fair is the system now?

Here are the major points on which fairness comes into play:

☐ AGE

If it's important to charge young people more for insurance, it could be done simply and efficiently, by computer. The computer that issues drivers' licenses already knows your birthday. It would just charge young drivers a higher license fee. That extra money would go into the insurance kitty and serve to reduce the amount that has to be collected at the pump.

But why bother with this?* It's true, young people as a group have more accidents.** But young people will grow old soon enough—it all evens out in the end.

What's more, the current system is unfair—and stupid. It penalizes good young drivers right along with the irresponsible ones. And it fines young drivers in advance, whether they drive safely or not. Their premiums can't go up much no matter how badly they drive, because they're already paying close to the highest rate.

Wouldn't it be smarter to penalize only those young drivers who drive recklessly, and thus give them an incentive not to? For example, instead of "fining" a young driver $800 in advance for being young, and $75 if he gets a speeding ticket, why not impose no fine for his age, but, say, $375 for a speeding ticket? Which is more likely to keep him from speeding?

---

*There are those who argue that high insurance rates for young drivers benefit society by discouraging them from driving. But the current system allows rich kids to drive, and tempts other kids to break the law. If we don't want young people to drive, why not just raise the age limit for a driver's license?

**Drivers under 25 represented 16% of the driving population in 1991, but 29% of all drivers involved in accidents. The record would be even more damning if it were based on fault rather than mere "involvement." But while strict equity demands that young drivers pay their disproportionate share of losses, it does not follow that they should also bear a disproportionate share of an insurer's expenses. It costs no more to sign up a young driver than an older one. Yet, typically, sales and overhead costs have been loaded into the premiums proportionally. Thus the urban male with a $1,500 premium may be paying $450 toward selling costs and overhead, while someone with a $150 premium pays only $45. This is unfair.

Under the current system, insurers must charge young people extra. It's not their fault—they'd go broke if they didn't.* But as a result, we're stuck with an unfair, stupid arrangement. Under PPN, this would be unnecessary. We could penalize only those who should be penalized—unsafe drivers—and do it in a way that provided a real incentive to drive safely.

❏ SEX

Women cause fewer serious accidents than men, and thus cost less to insure, in part simply because they drive fewer miles. Pay-at-the-Pump adjusts for this automatically, and so would be more fair than the current system, which does not.

But if the voters feel it's important to charge women still less (because they also tend to drive less aggressively than men, less often at night, and less often under the influence), so be it: a driver's sex is already noted by the computer on his or her license. It could just as easily spit out a bill that's $25 less for women than for men.

A fairness adjustment for sex serves little social purpose. It's not going to encourage anyone to drive more safely, or to switch sexes to get the lower rate. (An adjustment for airbags, by contrast, *would* encourage safety, by adding an incentive to buy them). But it could easily be done.

❏ MILES DRIVEN

Statistics show that the more you drive, the more likely you are to be involved in an accident, even if it's someone else's fault. So it stands to reason that people who drive a lot should pay more for auto insurance than people who don't.

The current auto insurance system does only a little to reflect this, and so is quite unfair. Pay-at-the-Pump, by contrast, reflects it very well: the more you drive, the more you pay.

❏ FUEL EFFICIENCY

Under PPN, gas guzzlers would pay more for insurance than others. But if that's deemed unacceptable, it could be handled automatically, efficiently, by an adjustment in automobile registration fees. The computer that spits out the annual auto registration bill already knows what kind of vehicle is being

---

*An insurer that didn't charge young people extra would be swamped with young customers. It would charge them all the "normal" rate, but then have to pay out claims at the "above-normal" rate at which young people have accidents.

registered (and every vehicle sold in the U.S. since 1974 has been assigned an EPA mileage rating), so it could easily be programmed to charge more for efficient models and less for guzzlers—or even to issue a rebate to guzzlers—if that's how the voters feel the system should work.

My own vote would be not to make an adjustment, given our common interest in encouraging a shift toward more efficient vehicles, and given that gas guzzlers contribute so much more than their share to environmental problems. But it could easily be done.

Note also that PPN won't be enacted overnight, and that those still driving low-mileage vehicles when it is will certainly be able to trade up to more efficient models. The market value of their old cars will, admittedly, decline somewhat with the higher price of gas. But it would make perfectly good sense for someone who drives a lot to trade his big old Lincoln for a more efficient model; and for someone who doesn't drive much but needs a car, or who needs an "extra" car for emergencies, to buy the Lincoln. (Under PPN, having a "back-up" car would be much less expensive than today, since the insurance premium would be next to nil if it were rarely driven.) With or without PPN, that's ideally what will happen: our newer, more efficient vehicles will do most of the work; our gas guzzlers will be held in reserve for the short hauls and occasional "overflow" duty. PPN would simply encourage this shift.

Note, too—and this applies to many of these areas of fairness—that a certain amount of equity is achieved simply because many people own more than one car, or care about more than one person, or see their circumstances change over time. What may be a hefty PPN charge to gas up Pop's Porsche may be balanced by the light freight on Mom's Miata. Son Bill may be paying through the nose on his two-ton 1977 Impala, but his fiancee Elaine may be tooling along at 50-miles-to-the-gallon in a Honda. To the extent people feel they are part of a larger family unit (even if its members don't all live together), many of the inequities may simply cancel each other . . . as they may, also, over time. Right now, you're commuting a long distance to work; but a year or two from now, you might transfer to a new location where you live right around the corner. Over a lifetime, it might well even out.

Note, finally, that at least with PPN you can partly control the cost of your insurance. Want to cut the cost in half? Buy a car that gets 25% better mileage. (You don't need to jump from 20 to 40 miles to the gallon to cut your cost in half, because when you save on PPN, by buying less gas, you save even more on the gas itself.)

☐ VEHICLE SAFETY

There's evidence that the biggest, heaviest cars—the ones that get the worst mileage—are the safest in a crash. *So they should be charged less.* On the other hand, they do the most damage in a crash, and so are the most dangerous to others. (Would you rather be hit by a Geo or a limo?) *So they should be charged more.* Big, heavy vehicles also tend to cost the most to repair. A new fender for a Cadillac or a Mercedes costs more than a new fender for a Chevy Cavalier.

What really seems to matter most in preventing serious injury—and huge insurance claims—isn't car size at all. It's whether the vehicle was equipped with air bags and whether the driver had his lap and shoulder belts fastened. (And who was driving. One reason stodgy old boats are safer than perky little imports is that stodgy old drivers tend to be behind the wheel. But they also tend to drive fewer miles, so under PPN, their premiums would be modest.)

In December, 1990, The Federal Highway Administration crashed a four-door Ford Taurus and a two-door Honda Civic into a pole. "Contrary to expectations," read the findings, "the larger car was less safe than the smaller car." In a separate test, the National Highway Traffic Safety Administration crashed an Isuzu Stylus head-on into a substantially larger Honda Accord. (A lot of Honda-bashing going on, if you ask me.) "The data from the instrumented dummies," reported *The Wall Street Journal*, "indicated that 'the small car occupant was safer than the large car occupant . . . probably due to the air bag present in the small car, but not in the larger vehicle.'"

In short, one wonders just how important it is to adjust insurance premiums to account for the safety and repairability of different makes and models. But the important point to make is that it could be done, efficiently, under PPN, just as with adjustments for fuel efficiency. High-risk vehicles could be surcharged at registration; low-risk vehicles could earn a discount.

(One thing it would make sense to encourage through adjustments at registration: airbags.)

☐ VEHICLE VALUE

We tend to think of auto theft and dented fenders as the main reason for auto insurance. This stands to reason, since the frequency of bashed headlights is much greater than the frequency of, say, quadriplegia. Actually, barely half the auto insurance premium we currently pay goes to insure cars. At least as much goes to cover the cost of insuring *people*. Still, property damage would be covered by PPN—fairly—and is the subject of Chapter 7.

☐ DRIVER'S INCOME

Under the current insurance system, an investment banker hurt in a crash will receive far more than a school-teacher, even though the teacher may have paid exactly the same premium and suffered exactly the same injuries. Is this fair?*

Is it fair to ask the $25,000-a-year driver to pay into the insurance pool enough to cover the $150,000-a-year driver's lost wages? Maybe yes, maybe no, but mark my words: given the choice between smashing into a 24-year-old med student and a 24-year-old bicycle messenger, you definitely want to hit the messenger. His life isn't "worth" nearly as much, and your liability will be much less.

PPN resolves this inequity. The basic coverage is for lost wages up to $25,000 a year. Young med students and others would be free to choose the $50,000 or $75,000 limit instead, sending in the additional premium due along with the rest of their annual registration fee. (For even more coverage, private disability insurance would be available, just as it is now.) But the school-teacher would no longer have to pay the extra cost of insuring the more valuable investment banker.

☐ URBAN/RURAL

In the first place, it's a myth that most accidents occur in the city. That may be true of routine scrapes, but not the really serious—and expensive—accidents. According to the National Safety Council, nearly two-thirds of all motor vehicle deaths occur in places classified as "rural"—28,100 fatalities in 1991 out of a total of 43,500. (One big reason: the higher speeds people travel outside congested areas. It's easy to dent a fender in a mall parking lot; harder, though not impossible, to kill someone. Another reason: a greater number of unlit, two-lane roads.)

Accidents do increase as traffic becomes more congested, but speed—and thus severity—decrease.

What's more, gas mileage suffers. A car that gets 30 miles to the gallon on rural highways might get only 10 or 15 in Manhattan, 3 or 4 on Boston's Southeast "Expressway."

---

*It works this way because the investment banker's economic damages—his lost wages—are much higher than the teacher's, so he can sue for much more.

Thus the need to compensate rural drivers for the greater distances they drive may not be as great as it at first appears. Rural drivers have more than their share of really serious, expensive accidents; and rural drivers get better gas mileage.

And there is a further point to be made: "[Urban] residents have to pay more for their auto insurance due to the fact that they live in more congested areas. Actually," writes Professor Michael Etgar, "the congestion is generated by suburban cars coming into the city." In San Francisco, for example, "almost every other person who works in the central city arrives there from one of the surrounding bedroom communities."*

So commuters should perhaps pay the higher urban rate. But it's more than that. In many cities, the surrounding population is relatively so large that the impact of even occasional visits by *non*commuters adds substantially to congestion.

The visitors may also be less familiar with city streets and driving conditions, a further hazard. They add to the conditions that make urban driving hazardous, with no practical way to charge them for doing so.

Thus, all things considered, it might not be so unfair, after all, if urban and rural drivers paid the same per-gallon auto insurance premium.

But to the extent an adjustment for fairness is required, there's a simple, efficient way to make it: vary the "deductible" amount depending on where an accident actually occurred. For example, you might lower the deductible by 50% in places the insurance industry currently classifies as rural; raise it by 50% in areas considered high risk. Under this automatic, efficient system, you'd strike a blow for fairness. And there's a bonus: you'd eliminate cheating. No longer could the city driver profit by fibbing and registering his car out in the sticks.

☐ DRIVING RECORD

Under the current system, many people with perfect driving records nonetheless pay high rates. This is unfair.

The efficient solution? Add an insurance surcharge to traffic fines. The simplest way: just double or even triple them, with the excess going straight to the insurance premium pool, to lower the price that would otherwise have to be charged at the pump.

---

*"Unfair Price Discrimination in P-L Insurance and the Reliance on Loss Ratios," *Journal of Risk and Insurance,* December 1975.

If a ticket now costs $75, it would cost $150 or even $225. The apparatus is already in place to issue tickets and collect fines. No new paperwork is required; just raise the fines.

The added advantage: a more direct incentive to drive safely.

As for penalizing the person who's repeatedly involved in minor accidents—a dent here and a dent there—the penalty would come three ways. First, in some cases the accident would result in a traffic ticket, with the attendant surcharge. Second, PPN includes a fairly high deductible, which would fall most heavily on the shoulders of the accident prone. Third, even without financial penalty, it's a major drag to be involved in any accident—even a small one. Perhaps that's penalty enough.

☐ ALTERNATIVE FUEL

Electric cars burn no gas, and thus would escape contributing to the PPN premium pool. The efficient solution is simply to add an insurance surcharge at registration each year.

☐ TAXIS

Taxicabs rack up a lot of mileage and would thus have huge insurance bills under PPN. But they already have huge insurance bills. It's unlikely they would pay more under PPN than they do now. If need be, however, an adjustment could be made (e.g., a nickel could be added to the cost of each ride).

☐ TRUCKS

Much the same could be said for trucks as for cabs, except they consume even more gas and probably are involved in fewer accidents. Then again, the accidents they *are* involved in can be horrendous. If need be, an efficient adjustment could be made (e.g., the current registration fee could be waived, with lost revenue to the state being made up by the revenue from the insurance pool). Or the increased cost, if any, could simply work its way through the system like any other added cost of doing business.

☐ MOTORCYCLES

To compensate for their extreme riskiness (and that noise) a $15,000 surcharge would be applied each year at registration. *Kidding!* But clearly, a high registration fee tied to the make and model of the cycle would be required, and/or PPN benefits might have to be cut—for example, the schedule of pain and suffering benefits might be eliminated (these guys are too tough to feel pain, anyway) and the lost-wage benefits reduced, in order to make the PPN registration fee affordable.

☐ LAWNMOWERS
If it costs an extra $4 a year to mow your lawn, because you're pouring PPN-priced gas into your lawnmower—tough! This is just not worth worrying about. (Well, conceivably, PPN could cover the unreimbursed medical expenses of people who accidentally mulched fingers or toes.)

☐ FARM EQUIPMENT
This is a much more serious issue. It takes very roughly 10 gallons of fuel to work an acre of ground, so an extra 35 or 40 cents a gallon on a typical 160-acre farm ain't hay. Even the relatively low federal and state gasoline excise taxes mount up—and are fully rebated to farmers in the form of an income tax credit. So the simplest way to exempt farmers from paying for PPN on their farm equipment would be to credit the full amount against their state income tax. (The state tax people would then get reimbursed for all these rebates, in a lump, out of the PPN premium pool.)

In states with no income tax, farmers would apply for the rebate direct from the insurance pool—attaching a copy of their federal tax return as proof of the number of gallons of gas they'd consumed.

☐ OUT-OF-STATE DRIVERS
The National Safety Council reports that 94% of all motor-vehicle accidents in 1991 occurred in the driver's home state. The percentage would be even higher in the kinds of states most likely to adopt PPN first—states like California, Texas, Florida and Hawaii—where relatively few people live within a short drive of a neighboring state. (New Jersey and Connecticut would be another matter.)

Still, for the relatively few accidents involving out-of-state drivers, two questions must be addressed. The first is: what do you do about out-of-state drivers?

One extreme would be to have them pay for PPN at the pump (though not at registration or licensing or in traffic-ticket surcharges), but not to give them anything in return. This would reduce the cost of PPN slightly for residents of the state, but surely not boost tourism.

The other extreme would be to cover an out-of-state driver with full benefits if he/she were involved in an accident in the state (even though he had paid nothing into the pool at registration, licensing or in traffic-ticket surcharges).

The fairest compromise might be partial coverage. In recognition that at least part of the gasoline that driver purchased may have been purchased inside the state, at PPN rates, and because out-of-state drivers *would* be subject to the traffic-ticket surcharges, out-of-state drivers would be covered for full medical reimbursement and lost wages to the extent his existing coverage fell short. Additionally, that driver would know that he/she could not be sued if he were involved in an accident in a PPN state.

□ DRIVING OUT OF STATE

The second question is, what do you do for a PPN-state resident who himself drives out of state? Eventually, of course, the hope is that all states would adopt PPN plans, and thus coverage could be standardized and universal. But in the meantime, it probably makes sense for PPN not to cover out-of-state accidents.

The main reason is to avoid fraud—namely, the temptation to register a vehicle in a PPN state, yet drive it, entirely or for the most part, outside the state. If PPN benefits extended out of state, such a driver would pay little or nothing for PPN (or any other auto insurance), yet be fully covered.

But—especially in the states most likely to adopt PPN first—very little driving *is* done out of state. And for those who do need such coverage, private policies would be readily obtainable. For example, just as Mutual of Omaha now sells travel-policies through vending machines at airports, so might daily and weekly auto insurance policies be available in vending machines at gas stations on either side of the border. (And for those who frequently drive out of state, private companies would doubtless fill the demand for policies that would cover out-of-state driving on an annual basis.)

□ BORDER PROBLEMS

Gas stations on the near side of the state border would be adversely affected until neighboring states, too, adopted PPN.

Part of the answer here is simply that progress brings a certain amount of dislocation. The same thing happens when a new highway opens—the gas stations and fast-food franchises on the old highway may see most of their business dry up. It's harsh but true.

Part of the answer may also lie in the revenue such near-border gas stations may earn selling out-of-state insurance policies, as just described. (It would make sense to buy such insurance on the near side of the border, even if you didn't buy gas, since otherwise you would be driving, for at least a brief period, uninsured—a misdemeanor in many states.) Or PPN might be written to cover drivers venturing up to 25 or 30 miles outside their state's border if they can show a valid credit-card receipt for having purchased gas within the prior 7 days on *this* side of the border. That would give them an incentive to gas up where they always have.

A small part of the answer may also lie in shared ownership. To the extent one person or company owns stations on *both* sides of the border, the dislocation would be less: the lost business on one side might be in large measure made up by the bonanza on the other side.

And a big part of the answer would come in encouraging neighboring states to adopt PPN more or less simultaneously. If it's good for California (and it is), it would probably be good for Arizona, Nevada, and Oregon, too.

To help near-border gas stations over the hump until neighboring states adopted a similar PPN charge, perhaps some limited subsidy or non-recourse low-interest loan might be made available. But it would be hard to justify this any more than one could justify subsidizing the McDonald's adjacent to an Army base or steel mill that shut down. With the rewards of being a small businessperson come the risks that something will happen that hurts or kills the business.

☐ THE POOR

As Robert Hunter, President of the National Insurance Consumer Organization (NICO) has pointed out, today the poor have a simple strategy: They drive uninsured. This is a reasonable, perhaps even a required economic choice for the poor, "judgment-proof" driver. (Why should he buy liability insurance to protect his assets when he has no assets to protect?) In inner cities, auto insurance can cost $1,000 or more even for accident- and ticket-free drivers. If the choice is to eat or buy auto insurance, it's an easy choice. In cities without good, affordable mass transit, like Los Angeles, almost everyone must own a car.

Pay-at-the-Pump would force the poor to buy insurance, but that may not be as cruel as it sounds.

In the first place, the cost under PPN would be far lower than it is today.

Second, auto insurance would actually become a lot more manageable for lower income people. It would be collected in small, affordable "installments," each time they bought gas. And no one would be denied coverage or face intimidating forms or be charged a high price based simply on where he or she lives.

Third, and so obvious as perhaps to be easily overlooked—they'd be covered! Far from driving with the knowledge they are breaking the law by driving uninsured, as now, they would be driving with the knowledge that, in the event of an accident, they'd be assured prompt reimbursement of medical costs and lost wages. This would be especially useful inasmuch as a disproportionate number of lower-income people lack health insurance.

Thus for today's poor-but-insured driver, PPN might provide a price break, and certainly increase coverage and make auto insurance easier to "buy" and pay for. Meanwhile, for today's *un*insured driver, PPN would provide two things he doesn't have now: coverage, plus relief from the anxiety over breaking the law—and facing severe penalties—each time he gets behind the wheel. (It's reasonable to believe that many uninsured motorists wish to be law abiding, and to have coverage. Under the current system, they just can't afford it.)

Still, a number of ideas have been proposed to lessen the impact of Pay-at-the-Pump on the currently-uninsured poor motorist. The most often mentioned: institute a "gas stamp" program for the poor. This is a dreadful idea, rife with bureaucracy, inefficiency, and the potential for fraud.

But there's something else that could be done—efficiently. It is a "self-certified discount" modeled on a successful energy subsidy in California. There, a utility-bill discount of about $50 a year is available to anyone with income below a certain level who simply certifies he is eligible for it. The combination of the low reward for cheating ($50), coupled with people's pride, integrity, and the potential penalties for signing a false statement, has made self-certification in California effective.

Borrowing from this idea, auto registration and licensing fees might be waived, in full or in part, for anyone who certifies his or her income is below a certain level. (To discourage cheating further, the self-certification form might include a field for the applicant's Social Security number, along with permission to obtain income verification from the IRS.) And the surcharge on traffic-tickets might be waived, as well. In one sense, it wouldn't be fair—rich drivers would subsidize poor ones. But fairness is in the eye of the beholder (or, in this case, the eye of the voter and his elected state representatives who would fine-tune and enact PPN). To some, it is only fair that the rich ease the insurance burden on the poor.

But whatever special treatment the poor were accorded, if any, it would surely be a benefit to all concerned to have currently uninsured drivers contribute *something* to the insurance pool, and to give them a way to "come in from the cold," respect the law, and be covered by adequate insurance.

The Bottom Line On Fairness

No insurance system is completely fair, least of all our current one.

For that matter, unfairness is everywhere in life. It costs 29 cents to send a first-class letter anywhere in the U.S. or Canada, regardless of distance or destination. In the interest of efficiency—not having a wildly complicated tariff structure—everyone pays the same.

HOW FAIR IS PPN?	
With respect to:	
AGE	More fair than now; and better incentives to drive safely
MILES DRIVEN	More fair than now; plus environmental benefits
FUEL EFFICIENCY	Less fair, but environmental benefits; or can be adjusted with registration surcharge/rebate.
DRIVER INCOME	More fair than now
VEHICLE VALUE	About the same; adjusted at registration and through deductibles
VEHICLE SAFETY	About the same, adjusted at registration
DRIVING RECORD	More fair than now; and better incentives to drive safely
URBAN/RURAL	About the same; and ends phony rural registration of urban vehicles
THE POOR	More fair than now; and a way for uninsured motorists to "come in from the cold"

Or think of this: small people subsidize large people. It costs more to make a large piece of clothing than a small one—more material, more stitching, higher shipping costs—yet large people normally pay no more for a shirt or a pair of shoes (or an airline ticket! or restaurant meals!) than small people.

What's *really* unfair about auto insurance isn't who winds up subsidizing whom, but how little of the money we collectively pay, as a society, goes for productive purposes, like fixing cars and healing bodies.

Under PPN, it would be up to each individual state to decide just how much fine-tuning to do. My own recommendation would be: not much. It's in the *nature* of insurance that some people subsidize others. But the beauty of PPN is that, to the extent you did want to fine-tune for fairness, you could do it effectively and efficiently. For just about *any* issue of equity—age, sex, driving record—an adjustment could be made efficiently, by computer, without adding a single bureaucrat or shuffling a single piece of paper.

Underwriting

Insurers don't just spend our money soliciting applications and deciding what rates to charge. They also spend our money deciding whom to reject.

Think of it! We require everyone to *buy* auto insurance, but then pay a cadre of bright people, called underwriters, to decide whom not to sell it to.

The Hartford Group, back when I researched *The Invisible Bankers*, was cautioning its underwriters against accepting airline stewardesses and construction workers, among others. Continental Insurance, while leery of advertising employees, caterers, and hairdressers, shunned "the swinger, the high flier, the ostentatious, the excessive entertainer, the celebrity, the slow payer, the excessive drinker or gambler (including amateur), the emotionally unstable and quick tempered, the exhibitionist, the jet set member, the divorce repeater and the just plain ornery."

Even clergy were considered to be a problem by many insurers, writes Robert Holtom.* "Often their minds are more on the concerns of their calling than on driving conditions. There was even a feeling by some underwriters that some clergy operated on the premise that God would take care of them, so they need not be bothered with traffic signals or other human restraints. Whatever the reasons, the

---

*Restraints on Underwriting: Risk Selection, Discrimination and the Law; The National Underwriter Co., 1979.

few studies which were made of actual loss experience by occupation indicated that clergy had among the highest loss ratios. ... Underwriters tended to reject the clergy."

From a single company's point of view, it may be good business to reject priests and rabbis, young people or caterers. But since we want everyone competent to drive to be able to do so, and to contribute something to the insurance pool rather than simply drive uninsured, why on earth spend money to reject their applications?

The irony is that, once the "bad risks" are weeded out, in many states they are thrown into an "assigned risk" pool, and often assigned to the very companies that rejected them. It's hard to imagine what value has been added by this circuitous process. Under PPN, it would simply disappear.

Mechanics

The mechanics of collecting premiums at the pump are simple. You'd just buy gas, as now, only it would cost 35 or 40 cents a gallon more.* A portion of what you paid would go to the state, just as it does now (the state gas tax). Only now the state's take would be much larger, as it would include not just the state tax, but also the insurance premium.

The state would deposit the money it receives into two accounts: the account for the gasoline tax, as now, and a new account, controlled by the state Insurance Department, for the insurance premium.

The mechanics of adding a young-driver surcharge to the driver's license fee, or a high-risk-vehicles surcharge at registration, are equally simple. Likewise, adding a premium to moving-violation fines. In each case, the excess money collected would go into the Insurance Department premium pool.

But as explained in the next chapter, the state Insurance Department wouldn't keep the money. This is pay-at-the-pump *private* no-fault auto insurance.

---

*In states like Minnesota, where the accident rate per mile is low, the premium might be more like 25 cents.

QUESTIONS

25. How would the premiums be collected?

Efficiently. The plan is called "pay-at-the-pump," but actually there are four efficient collection points: the gas pump, the driver's license fee, the license plate and the traffic ticket. They are "efficient" because they are already in place. Virtually no new effort or paperwork would be required to collect the premium this way—and a tremendous amount of effort would be saved if we did.

26. I don't get it. How would the gas station attendant know what to charge me? Would there be a separate form to fill out every time I filled my tank?

Hello? Anybody home? This is not the way it would work. You'd just fill up your tank as you normally do. Everyone would pay the same insurance-premium-per-gallon, just as everyone pays the same state and federal gasoline tax.

27. Who would collect the insurance money from the gas station?

The same people who already collect the state gasoline tax. Not a single new government employee would be required.

28. Whoa! What if I just paid my $600 semi-annual premium the day before this plan went into effect?

There'll be plenty of warning before PPN is enacted, and those who still had time to run on their existing policies would get a pro-rata rebate.

29. If PPN's higher gas price got people to use less gas, wouldn't the price-per-gallon have to rise even higher?

Yes. And wouldn't that be great? If over time PPN helped us burn, say, 15% less gas, we'd have to raise the PPN premium 15% to stay even. But we'd also be buying 15% less gas, and so would wind up, overall, way ahead. (The overall cost of PPN would remain the same—a higher price on fewer gallons; but we'd be spending 15% less on the gas itself, and that would save us money.) What's more, we'd have cut down on the environmental costs we all share, and perhaps even cut down a bit on traffic jams and accidents, as well as the trade deficit and on our dependence on foreign energy.

30. If agents can't sell auto insurance, won't they just raise the price of everything else?

No. With rent to pay and a payroll to meet, you certainly couldn't blame insurance agencies for *wanting* to replace lost auto insurance premiums by raising other premiums. But agents don't set rates—insurers do. And in a competitive marketplace, it's not easy to raise prices.

Something else is likely to happen: The industry would consolidate.

Seeing PPN on the horizon, big agencies might begin shrinking by attrition and, eventually, if need be, laying people off. With far less work to do, there simply wouldn't be the need for so many employees. Smaller agencies might merge, the better to share the overhead. Some clerical workers might go into nursing (where there is a strong demand). Some auto insurance specialists might develop expertise in new lines of insurance—computer fraud, and data integrity, for example, where their efforts *can* add value.

In a free economy, these things sort themselves out. Change is always painful, but in the long run, efficiency makes almost everyone richer.

31. Where do you come up with your energy conservation estimates?

It stands to reason that higher priced gas would cut consumption at least a little. That's simple supply-and-demand economics. The question is: how much?

In an extensive report to the State of California Energy Resources Conservation and Development Commission in May, 1990, economist Mohamed M. El-Gasseir estimated that each 10% increase in the cost of gas would lead to a 2% decline in consumption in the short run, as people drove more efficiently (a little more carpooling, a little better planning to avoid unnecessary trips, a little better attention to tune-ups and tire air-pressure, occasionally taking the bus) and 7% in the long run (mainly through the purchase of more efficient cars). Thus a 40-cent PPN premium which raised the cost of gas 30% would lower consumption by about 6% in the short-run, if these projections are accurate, and perhaps 20% or more in the long run. *No one would be forced to do anything he didn't want to do, and for most people the overall cost of driving would go down.* Yet by paying premiums at the pump instead of through the mail, we'd be sending the right economic signals, and getting people to "want" to do something that makes more sense for everybody: burn less fuel.

32.   Wouldn't the price per gallon rise with inflation?

Yep. Maybe even a little faster than inflation, if health care costs continue to outstrip inflation. But that's exactly what's been happening with our current system of auto insurance, and will continue to happen unless we change it. Relatively speaking, the savings would still be there—magnified all the more by inflation.

33.   How can PAY-AT-THE-PUMP provide so much more in benefits at such low cost?

Under the current system, insurers and their agents must deal, one on one, with 200 million separate vehicles. Under the new system, all 200 million would be covered automatically. Insurers would have to deal only with the much smaller number involved in accidents. After all, what useful service does an insurer render a policyholder until he has a claim? Beyond that, PPN would eliminate the lawyers, eliminate duplicate payments (why reimburse someone twice for the same medical bill?) and eliminate "lottery-type" pain and suffering benefits (though people would be free to purchase such policies separately) in favor of what most people really need: prompt, sure coverage for all unreimbursed medical expenses and lost wages.

34.   But isn't this ... well, socialist?

Not any more than group health insurance or unemployment insurance or worker's comp.

Insurance is *itself* a cooperative enterprise, a sharing of risk. Much of our insurance is *already* provided in group, state-wide or even national plans. Beyond that, a huge chunk is provided by mutuals. Mutual insurers, while stanchions of capitalism, are nonetheless at root socialist institutions, owned not by capitalists but (in theory at least) by "the people" (i.e., the policyholders). So it would be a little silly to deny ourselves an efficient, equitable auto insurance system on the grounds that it were somehow unAmerican.

And, as I say, PPN would still be very much a *private* insurance system.

Chapter 4

PRIVATE
(No Government)

The same private enterprise insurance companies that settle auto insurance claims now would continue to do so under PPN. Only, because the system would be a little different, some of the least efficient companies would contract or merge, and those that remained would have an incentive to provide even better service than they do now.

(Not everyone is thrilled with the way auto insurers handle claims now, but what is the alternative? Do you want the *government* setting up a bureaucracy to settle insurance claims?)

Right now, an auto insurer competes for business partly on price and service, partly on marketing expenditures and skills. Under PPN, only price and service would count.

And right now, a large portion of an insurer's profit depends on how skillfully it can distinguish the "good risks" from the "bad risks," either shunning the bad risks altogether, or charging them an appropriately high rate. For any given company, this is a crucial job and an exciting intellectual challenge. But for society as a whole, because we want everyone to carry auto insurance, it is a total waste of effort.

Under PPN, all risks would be equal—each block of 5,000 insured vehicles would be statistically identical to any other. So rather than have to make 5,000 underwriting decisions for each individual vehicle in the group—or even hundreds of actuarial analyses, one for each block of 5,000 vehicles—insurers would need to make a single (important) judgment: how much is it likely to cost to settle all the claims of any given 5,000-vehicle group?

Insurers are very good at figuring these things out. And because of the "law of large numbers," it's not that hard to come pretty close. The number of auto accidents does not rise and fall dramatically from year to year—to see this, check out the table of motor vehicle fatalities on the facing page. There are a few "bumps" in the numbers, but mostly favorable ones, that would increase insurance company profits (for example, accidents and fatalities drop noticeably during recessions*). By and large, the numbers are fairly predictable—not for any single family, but for large numbers of people—and the trend is generally down. More than 2.8 million Americans have died in fatal auto accidents since the first one in 1899, but with any luck the annual death toll may have peaked in 1972. Even though more miles are driven almost every year, the number of fatalities—and severely disabling accidents—gradually falls, the result, mainly, of the gradual shift to safer cars and better roads.

Of course, the preponderance of auto accidents are not fatal. In 1991, there were approximately 1.6 million "disabling" injuries (defined as any injury that kept you from doing your normal activities beyond the day of the accident itself). But the estimated average cost of each fatal injury in 1991 was $450,000, compared to an average of just $20,300 for each nonfatal-but-disabling injury (and $4,200 for each non-disabling accident).

The point is, accidents happen randomly to you and me, but predictably over large numbers, and the insurance companies will be able to make good guesses as to what it will cost to handle a block of business in any given state.

Under PPN, the guesses would be a little hard to make the first year or two, because no one would know for sure exactly how much would be saved in such things as the greatly decreased incentive to "build" claims. So at first insurers might be expected to err on the high side. But pretty soon, cost estimates would become quite sharp, and bidding for blocks of business, intense.

---

*When times are tough, people cut back on entertaining and socializing, especially on Saturday nights, the worst time for accidents, and there's less commuting to work, because fewer people are working.

MOTOR VEHICLE FATALITIES

Year	Deaths
1915	6,800
1925	21,800
1935	36,369
1945	28,076 - young drivers off at war
1955	38,426
1965	49,163

Year	Deaths
1970	54,633
1971	54,381
1972	56,278
1973	55,511
1974	46,402 - 55 MPH speed limit imposed
1975	45,853
1976	47,083
1977	49,510
1978	52,411
1979	53,524
1980	53,172
1981	51,385
1982	45,779 - recession
1983	44,452
1984	46,263
1985	45,901
1986	47,865
1987	48,290
1988	49,078
1989	47,575
1990	46,800
1991	43,500 - recession

Source: National Safety Council

The insurers that bid the least—who offered to cover blocks of business at least cost—would win the right to do so, with three caveats:

First, to avoid wild and inefficient swings in market share (it would hardly be efficient to have State Farm laying off half its claims managers one year, only to have to rehire them the next!), the maximum number of blocks any one insurer could bid on and win in a given year would be related to the amount of business it was previously doing in the state. For example, a limit of 5%-a-year additional market share might be imposed, meaning that if right now State Farm were insuring 30% of the states vehicles and GEICO just 3%, the first year under PPN State Farm would not be allowed to win more than 35% of the blocks, and GEICO might not be allowed to win more than 8%.

Second, the maximum number of blocks any given insurer could win would depend on how well it had scored that year with its claimants. Those with above-average "Customer Satisfaction" ratings would be allowed to win more blocks. Those below-average ratings would see their maximum allowable market share shrink. For details on the Customer Satisfaction ballot, see Chapter 6.

Third, as now, the state Insurance Departments would have to be satisfied of an insurer's financial strength before it would be allowed to expand its share of the market.

So there would not be wild gyrations in market share. But there would be constant pressure toward awarding business to the lowest-priced insurers that provided the most satisfactory claims settlements.

What's more, PPN would allow for easier entry into the auto insurance business. With no sales and marketing apparatus required, and with no risk of the freak $15 million lottery-style award to scare them off, new, more efficient competitors might appear. For example, an association of state Exxon dealers might form a corporation with a private hospital chain and bid for blocks of business. So long as the new organization could show adequate financial reserves, they would be allowed to bid just as Travelers does. And it just might be that auto mechanics are better at controlling repair costs, and hospitals better at controlling medical costs, than traditional insurance companies.

GM's Mr. Goodwrench might get into the auto insurance business in a big way as a spirited competitor. And if he did, GM would have an added incentive to build safe cars that are cheap to repair and hard to steal.

Or Sears, which owns Allstate Insurance but also a chain of auto-repair locations, might bid aggressively on blocks of business and, where possible, perform repairs itself. (It might offer claimants some small but real incentive—perhaps a free $25 or $50 gift certificate at the adjoining Sears store—to encourage them to chose Sears repair.) So much for repair fraud: since it would only be defrauding itself, there would be little point in overcharging for repairs.

The more bidders, the better.

How much of this would the average driver have to know about or understand? *None of it.* In the event of an accident, he'd simply call the 800-number on his registration and file the claim. Once the settlement was reached, he'd take an extra couple of minutes to fill out and send in his Customer Satisfaction ballot.

And though it sounds a little complicated for insurers, and for the state Insurance Departments, it's nowhere near as complicated as the system now. Under the current system, a California applicant to State Farm will be assigned one of over 5 million rates, depending on which of four categories matches his or her driving record, which of 92 driver categories he or she fits (determined mostly by mileage driven and years of driving experience), which of the 57 combinations of claim frequency zones and claim cost regions applies to the area where the policyholder resides, and to which of over 252 categories his or her vehicle is assigned ($4x92x57x252 = 5,285,952$). And under the current system, state Insurance Departments go nuts trying to fathom auto insurance company accounting to determine whether unacceptable profits are being made, or unacceptable risks being assumed. Under PPN, *all* profits would be acceptable—the competitive bidding process would be enough to keep them in line. And under PPN, the overall riskiness of the business would be less (because without lawyers, the average cost of each claim would be lower, and the chance of some freak monster award, nil), so there would be somewhat less concern for the financial health of the insurer (though it would still be important to allow only financially qualified insurers to bid).

Profit is a good thing, not a bad thing, and under PPN insurers would be entirely free—much freer than now, in many states—to make it.

QUESTIONS

35. You mean I couldn't choose my own insurer? I *love* State Farm!

Sorry. You could choose State Farm for any additional coverage you might want to buy, but as with group health insurance, you don't get to choose which insurer covers you. Still, this may not be as bad as it sounds. One reason some people love their auto insurers is not that they get good service but simply that they get a good price. With PPN, almost everyone would get a good price.

The paradox is that the more you love your insurer because it gives you prompt, full payments every time you make a claim, the closer you are to having your rates hiked or your coverage dropped! Very few insurers go on forever paying claim after claim after claim.

With PPN, your rates could *not* be raised for filing a claim (though you could get a whopper of a ticket if the accident had been the result of a moving traffic violation), and neither could your coverage be dropped. And because the companies that scored best in the Customer Satisfaction ranking would be given an edge in the bidding, the odds would be skewed in favor of your being covered by an insurer that served you well.

36. What if it *didn't* serve me well.

You'd complain, as now. You'd give it lousy grades on the Customer Satisfaction ballot. And in truly egregious cases, as now, you would go to the state Insurance Department or sue for bad faith.

37. What if I truly hated my insurer?

In the real world, I suppose there will people who just go nuts that their block of business had been won by some particular insurer. Perhaps the insurer treated him or one of his relatives horribly in years past.

It hardly seems worth the effort, but if states wanted to, they could include a special provision by which a driver who had some special reason for wanting to be reassigned to "anyone but" his present insurer could be, at the discretion of the Insurance Department and for a modest processing fee.

38. What would PPN do to insurance companies?

It would hurt the inefficient companies but provide exciting opportunities for the efficient ones. Overall, it would require lay-offs or reassignments, because far fewer people would be required to provide coverage—even though it would be better coverage than we have now. Almost all the marketing and underwriting people would be freed up for more productive work; almost all the attorneys who handle claims would be unnecessary.

39.   What about agents?
The "professional commitment statement" of the Chartered Property Casualty Underwriter says in part that he "will strive to ascertain and understand the needs of others and place their interest above [his] own." Not all auto insurance agents have earned the CPCU designation, but for those who have, PPN will be a severe test of their commitment. Just as it's tough for a weapons specialist to be for disarmament, or a dentist to be for an end to tooth decay, so it can't be easy for auto insurance agents to support a system that cuts deeply into their livelihood.

However, it should be noted that many property/casualty insurance agents sell far more than just auto insurance—homeowners and business insurance, for example—and that even under PPN there would remain some demand for individual policies to cover the deductibles and lottery-type pain and suffering awards PPN doesn't.

But no question: if your son or daughter is thinking of becoming an auto insurance salesperson, he or she'd be wise to think twice. (See also, Question #30.)

40.   Wouldn't some "blocks" be more attractive than others?
No. That would be true if they were assigned by zip code or vehicle-type, or perhaps even by birthday (who knows: people born in December might be better risks than people born in June). But under PPN, each vehicle would be assigned to a block *at random*, so all blocks would be statistically alike. This is an easy thing for a computer to do, and every state in the union has long since computerized its auto registration process.

41.   How do you keep the politicians' hands out of the pot?
Good question! But there is a good answer, and it is ironclad: The cash from the pump (and from the licensing, registration, and traffic-ticket surcharges) would go straight to a bank account controlled by the State Insurance Department. The Law establishing PPN would clearly state that this account is inviolate. Most of the funds would go out to insurers just as fast as it came in—winning

bidders would be paid their winning bid on a weekly or monthly basis. And the relatively small "float" and surplus that would be retained in the account to keep the system working smoothly would simply be, as a matter of law, out of bounds.

42. How do you assure that the bidding is handled fairly?

There are two things to worry about here. The first is that state Insurance Department officials might somehow be bribed to favor an inferior bidder. But the law would provide for disclosure of all bids after each auction, so the low bids would be plain to see. If Allstate saw that it should have won blocks of business that went instead to another insurer, it would protest loudly. Furthermore, the guidelines by which companies with high Customer Satisfaction scores would be favored in the bidding would be clearly spelled out and disclosed well in advance (see Chapter 6)—they would not be decided subjectively after the bids were in, or manipulated from year to year. Finally, Insurance Department expertise would be required in deciding whether an insurer had the requisite financial strength to bid on all the business it wanted to, and in this area—as now—we would simply have to rely on the integrity and expertise of the Department staff (which are generally considerable).

The second worry would be collusion among bidders. What if they all met out on the golf course, winked, and rigged the bids. This is always possible (though under our criminal anti-trust statutes it could expose those golfers to lengthy jail terms*), but with as many potential bidders as there would be—scores of companies write auto insurance, and still more might be eager to under PPN—it would be hard to do. Still, the Insurance Department and the financial press would have every reason to be on the look-out for signs of collusive bidding.

43. How do you set the premium-at-the-pump initially, to be sure it's high enough?

Just as insurers can make a good guess as to what their costs under PPN will be, so can the Insurance Department. To be on the safe side, and to build a modest surplus to avoid having to raise the premium with each uptick in inflation, it would be wise to start

---

*Actually, there's a small problem here. Since 1944, when the insurance industry got Congress to pass the McCarran-Ferguson Act, it has been largely exempt from federal regulation, including the anti-trust laws. For the PPN bidding process to work, it would have to be clear that McCarran-Ferguson does not apply to collusive bidding, or else states would have to follow California's lead and subject insurers to anti-trust laws of their own.

high—45 cents might make sense if 40 cents appears likely to do the trick. Another way to build a little cushion is to begin collecting the extra premium a month or two before PPN coverage actually kicks in.

But even if, worst case, results of the bidding showed that an even higher premium would be required initially, until insurers saw the large profits they could make and thus began to bid more aggressively, the program should not be perceived to have failed. Right now, as explained at the outset of Chapter 3, the average insured American driver is paying the equivalent of about 85 cents a gallon for his auto insurance. And if nothing changes, that's likely to keep marching right on up and up. So if the PPN premium turned out to be 50 cents instead of 40 cents or 35 cents, it would not be the end of the world.

The thing to remember is that there's *no way*, if you cut out the lawyers and the sales costs and the duplicated payments, and so on, we could possibly pay more for auto insurance under PPN than we do under the current system, or get less back for our premium dollar than we do now. Anyone who tells you otherwise is just trying to confuse the issue to protect his own little pot of gold.

44. Who would get the investment income?

We pay for auto insurance two ways. First, in the check we write, which is the obvious part; but second, in turning over the use of our money to the insurance company for what may be a long, long time. That's a hidden payment we make, but it is very significant to the auto insurers. They get our premium dollar now, but may not have to make the final claim payment for many years.

Under PPN, insurers' float would decrease somewhat, because without lawyers, and with a set schedule for pain and suffering benefits, etc., claims would be settled a lot faster. Still, there would definitely be premium dollars to invest, and the winning bidders would profit from investing it, just as they do now.

But far from begrudging insurers that profit, we'd hope it's huge—because the greater the potential investment income, the more eager insurers will be to win blocks of business, and the lower will be their bids. An insurer that believed it could make a profit covering a block of 5,000 California vehicles for $2.5 million might see that, because of likely investment income, it could offer to handle the business for just $2.3 million. Bully for them. Bully for us.

45. If no one can be turned down for insurance, What about fraud?
This is an important point. A huge portion of our auto insurance
premium dollar today goes to paying padded and fraudulent claims.
Under PPN, it would be important to mitigate that problem, not
make it worse.

Fraud would be combated, as now, by insurers. Under PPN, they
would continue to have a selfish incentive not to pay fraudulent
claims—the fewer they paid, the more money they would get to
keep.

Industry-wide efforts, like those of the Insurance Crime
Prevention Institute, (recently merged with the National
Automobile Theft Bureau to form the National Insurance Crime
Bureau), would continue or—better still—be enhanced.

But PPN *by its very nature* would do a lot to help. By eliminating
lawyers, you eliminate the problem that some of them are crooked.
By eliminating the practice of paying "three times" actual damages
by way of pain and suffering, you eliminate the incentive to "build"
the claim. How much fun are unnecessary visits to the chiropractor
if you're not getting paid to make them? By building in significant
deductibles, you eliminate millions of minor claims, some of which
would inevitably be padded. By setting the standard for collision
repairs more sensibly (see Chapter 7), and thus not attempting to
make an older vehicle "good as new," you eliminate some of the
ability to pad bills and some of the incentive to use the insurance
system as an all-purpose auto-repair fund.

And note that for "extra" coverages—coverage for the deductible
amount and extra pain-and-suffering coverage—insurers *would* be
able to turn down applicants they felt they could not trust to make
honest claims.

**46. What do you mean "no government"? It sounds like there'd be
plenty of government!**
That's true—but no more than now. The state Insurance
Department (and every state already has one) would simply
supervise the competitive bidding process, a very important job but
not a very big one, and then funnel the PPN proceeds through to
the winning bidders as they're received. It would also need to
contract with some well-respected private outfit to tabulate the
results of the Customer Satisfaction balloting in advance of the
bidding each year.

Actually, it might be a good idea for the Insurance Department
to contract the whole thing to some independent and highly

professional third party like a Big Six accounting firm. And to retain a couple of local business school professors for two- or three-year terms to oversee the process generally, and keep an eye out for possible improvements. But either way, in the scheme of things, not a lot of cost or people would be involved. And remember: the Insurance Department already has people answering questions and complaints. Under PPN, which is simpler, there might be fewer questions (at least after the first year or two). And under PPN, which should involve a much less contentious claims settlement process, there might be fewer complaints.

What's really meant by "no government" is simply that the huge auto insurance job that does need doing—settling the claims and investing the premiums in the meantime—would be done by private enterprise, just as it is now.

Chapter 5

NO-FAULT
(No Lawyers)

Accidents happen.

A friend of mine was driving his old '84 Honda up New York's West Side Highway on his way up to Connecticut. Chester, his golden retriever, was in back. Suddenly, the driver ahead of him stopped short. He had stopped, he later told my friend, because he could see, a few cars ahead, a car cutting off another and an accident about to ensue. "Unfortunately," recalls my friend, "I was going up a small slope and couldn't see that he had stopped until too late.

"Actually, it was barely too late. Had we been on even ground, our bumpers would have bumped without damage. Instead, mine went under his. His car was undamaged; mine had some front-end damage. The collision wasn't strong enough to make his car hit the one ahead of him.

"His wife was hysterical at first, screaming that I had imperiled their baby . . . but once she realized the baby was tranquil in its car-seat, she calmed down. Her husband, a cheerful guy, said he had been watching my wide-eyed face in his rear-view mirror. He said he didn't think I'd be able to brake in time—and of course he was right. But since his car was undented, he seemed unperturbed.

"In front of us, four cars had been involved in a collision—one of them totaled—triggered by the guy who had cut into the lane. That car—totally unscathed—waited a minute and then sped off. I took down the license number.

"Soon, an ambulance arrived, which I guess is standard procedure whenever there's a crack-up like this. The driver checked with everybody and found no one needed anything, except Chester, who was thirsty. He gave Chester some sterilized in a bedpan, and then left.

"The car of the man who caused the accident and drove away didn't seem badly dented, but I only saw it for a few seconds so I can't be sure. It was a late model livery car—you know, not a limo but maybe a 1990 or 1991 Lincoln, something like that—driven, I later learned, by a Russian immigrant. I learned his name only when the court papers arrived, asserting that he'd been injured in the accident and was suing me, along with everyone else in the chain."

There were ten defendants named in the lawsuit (including spouses), residing variously in Connecticut, New Jersey, Massachusetts, Manhattan, Brooklyn, Long Island and the Bronx. Several separate insurance companies were involved.

"I told my insurance agent that not only had the livery driver (1) *caused* the accident and (2) left the scene of the accident, but that, most relevantly, since the car I hit had hit no other car, and since I was the last car in the chain, I couldn't possibly have had any involvement with his injuries, whatever they might be."

Still, a year has passed and all parties to the suit are busily doing all the things parties to a lawsuit do. Paper is flying around the tri-state region, most recently an "answer with cross claim" filed by one of the ten defendants' lawyer's, denying, in its first paragraph, any knowledge "sufficient to form a belief as to the allegation(s) contained in paragraph(s) designated as 'FIRST, SECOND, THIRD, FOURTH, FIFTH, SIXTH, SEVENTH, EIGHTH, NINTH, TENTH, ELEVENTH, TWELFTH, THIRTEENTH, FOURTEENTH, FIFTEENTH, SIXTEENTH, SEVENTEENTH, EIGHTEENTH, NINETEENTH, TWENTIETH, THIRTY-THIRD, THIRTY-FOURTH, THIRTY-FIFTH, THIRTY-SIXTH, FORTY-THIRD and FORTY-SIXTH' of the complaint herein," with additional paragraphs and documents denying other things, all neatly legal—copies of all of which were sent by this co-defendant to all the other co-defendants and, of course, to the plaintiff and filed with the court. *AGGGGGGGH!*

My friend is presumably in no real danger of any kind—his insurance company is handling his defense. But it's still no fun to be sued, no fun to have a pending lawsuit show up on one's credit record. "My main worry," says my friend, "is that to avoid the risk and bother of a court case, the insurance company will give some money to the reckless driver and his unspeakable lawyer."

That's how auto insurance works now. (And this was in New York, which is one of the supposed "no-fault" states!)

Who is paying for all these lawyers? Under the current system, *you* are.

Lawyers, as a group, have never been much more popular than insurance companies, and yet in America's litigious soil they have flourished, twining a tangled, strangling and near impenetrable mesh. Some of my best friends are lawyers—and they agree. Thirty thousand new lawyers enter the mainstream each year (like beavers, preparing to clog it up). There are more lawyers in the U.S. than in the rest of the world combined. And it is in the direct interest of at least one lawyer in almost any lawsuit to stall.

For an accident victim, the quicker the case can be settled, the faster will be his psychological and physical recovery. "It has always been axiomatic in medical circles," writes Professor Jeffrey O'Connell, "that promptness is essential to good medical treatment of trauma. The victim must be made to put the accident behind him." Yet the insurance system is designed not for the victims but for the lawyers. Far from putting the accident behind them, victims are instructed to keep detailed diaries of their pain and disability—an hourly account of what hurts and what they are prevented from doing. Sometimes they will even forgo rehabilitation, consciously or unconsciously trying to "prove" that their claim for pain and suffering is worthy. It would hardly do, after all, to get up before a jury all smiles and in the peak of health. And yet the trial may come only years after the accident. O'Connell (who is widely known as "the father of no-fault insurance") quotes a colleague who calls this "the schizophrenic choice between 'recovery' in the medical sense and 'recovery' in the legal sense." And he concludes: "Given the purposes of the tort liability system, lawyers cannot be blamed for thus advising their clients. But many in the medical profession are understandably shocked by a system that, contrary to all medical wisdom, encourages accident victims to preserve, hug, and indeed nurture and memorialize every twinge and hurt from an accident."

Nothing supports lawyers like insurance. No wonder lawyers, who control the legal system, have fought so hard, and with great success, against "no-fault" insurance. No fault, no lawsuits. No lawsuits, no lunch.

No-Fault Auto Insurance

The reform that fairly screams to be made is the institution of true no-fault automobile insurance. No-fault would be of great benefit to almost everyone but the lawyers.

Today, most serious auto accident victims are terribly undercompensated for their medical expenses and lost wages.
The dream of a huge award for pain and suffering is, for almost all, only a dream. And whatever large sums *are* awarded are heavily taxed by the lawyers.*

Traditional auto liability insurance was long ago characterized in a report by the New York State Insurance Department as "the worst system imaginable: A system that not only fails to spread most of [the] loss but is cruel, corrupt, self-righteous, dilatory, expensive and wasteful." It overcompensates petty and groundless claims, because they are too expensive to fight, and grossly undercompensates the seriously injured, and then only after much delay. Each time a $500 case is settled for $1,200, to get rid of it, insurers are in effect paying a "toll" to lawyers for letting them pass without a lawsuit. Even when no attorney is involved, it is protection money, paid under threat that the claimant *could* retain an attorney. Settling petty or groundless claims for several times their economic value (medical expenses and lost wages) leaves too little of the insurance dollar for the people who really need it.

With no-fault, the idea is to get an accident victim reimbursed promptly and as fully as possible for medical expenses and lost wages. In return for sure, swift compensation, the policyholder gives up his right to sue.

---

*A survey of 60,000 accident victims and 29 insurers published in 1979 by the All-Industry Research Advisory Committee, an insurance-industry organ, found that, under the current system, "persons with economic losses [medical and lost wages] up to $2,500 received payments of more than $2 for every $1 of economic loss" while those with losses above $10,000 received less than $1 for each $1 of loss—*before* paying their attorneys and *after* taking into account health insurance payments other than auto insurance coverage. Although the dollar amounts would have about doubled since then because of inflation, there's no reason to think much else has changed: minor injuries get overcompensated; serious ones—the ones that really matter—go undercompensated.

The study also found that under fault systems, only about 46% of the claimants had begun receiving insurance payments within 90 days of notifying the insurance company of their injuries. Under no-fault systems, the comparable figure was 81%. (Interestingly, the study also found that under a "fault" insurance system, claimants with economic losses under $500 received more from the system if they were represented by an attorney, even after paying the estimated attorney fees. But *"claimants with economic losses greater than $2,000 received a larger net return if they were not represented by an attorney."* Also, "Attorney-represented claims took considerably longer to settle than nonrepresented claims. For BI [bodily injury] claims, those with attorneys took an average of 500 days from the first report of injury to the final payment, compared with an average of 100 days for nonrepresented claims.")

True no-fault auto insurance eliminates the potential bonanza for a man struck down by a chauffeur-driven Rolls-Royce, but eliminates, too, the current norm: woefully inadequate payments, much disputed and long delayed. It assumes that accidents are, by and large, just that—accidents, not intentional assaults—and that society's effort should be primarily directed not at finding fault but at aiding the victim. Indeed, in many auto injury cases more professional hours are logged by lawyers than doctors!

"The courts are overwhelmed, swamped, inundated, choked," New York Senator Daniel Patrick Moynihan has written. "In a futile quest to carry out a mundane mission—deciding who hit whom on the highway when every day there will be thousands and thousands of such events. . .—we are sacrificing the most precious of our institutions: the independent judiciary, which dispenses justice and maintains the presumption and perception of a just social order that is fundamental to a democratic political system."

Take a minute to read what one well-known consumer advocate (initials RN) wrote about no-fault auto insurance as a young lawyer way back when: "In the days of poor roads and low speeds," he wrote, "the fact of an accident could be reconstructed in a courtroom with some degree of accuracy, and the problem of determining fault did not present unusual difficulties. But with high-powered cars and concrete highways, the probability that an accident—often the consequence of a fractional mistake in management—can and will be described accurately in court has become increasingly remote, especially where court congestion has delayed the time of trial." That was Richard Nixon, in 1936. Nixon came to that conclusion. Moynihan, on the other side of the political spectrum, came to that conclusion. Almost *everybody* comes to that conclusion, with just a few exceptions.

Oddly, one of the most troubling of these exceptions is that other RN, Ralph Nader. Given his unique position as America's leading consumer advocate, this is unfortunate—and, one hopes, subject to change. Nader recoils from any restriction on the Little Guy's access to the courts, because he sees it as consumers' only practical defense against the big guys. And he's probably right. But the lawsuits no-fault would rule out aren't the ones against the big guys. They are the lawsuits between two drivers who got into an accident.

The No-Fault Numbers

True no-fault auto insurance allows a much larger proportion of each premium dollar to reach the accident victim. Fair, fast and efficient, it was recommended to the nation by a team from Columbia University as long ago as 1932. But the fight for no-fault only got under way in earnest in the late 1960s. To the casual observer, the fight would seem to have been won. Many states today have one or another form of no-fault insurance. But in all of them there is a threshold of damages—often low—beyond which the fault system takes over and victims can sue. That has merely encouraged victims and their lawyers to incur unnecessary medical expenses in order to "build up the claim," exceed the threshold and thus qualify to sue for pain and suffering.

No-Fault In Name Only	
State	**Threshold Above Which You Can Sue**
Colorado	$ 500
Connecticut	$ 400
Florida	*verbal*
Hawaii	*verbal*
Kansas	$2000
Kentucky	$1000
Massachusetts	$2000
Michigan	*verbal*
Minnesota	$4000
New Jersey	*choice*
New York	*verbal*
North Dakota	$2500
Pennsylvania	*choice*
Utah	$3000

Verbal thresholds are based on a description of the severity of the injury, not a dollar amount. New Jersey and Pennsylvania offer a choice of no-fault or fault systems.

A report issued in 1970 by the New York State Insurance Department assailed the efficiency of the traditional auto liability insurance system. "What becomes of the personal injury liability insurance dollar?" the report asked, answering:

First of all, insurance companies and agents use up 33 cents. Then lawyers and claims investigators take the next 23 cents. Together these items make up the operating expenses, or frictional costs, of the fault insurance system—56 cents out of every premium dollar.

What happens to the 44 cents that get through to the accident victim?

First, 8 cents of the 44 go to pay for economic losses that have already been reimbursed from another source. Subtracting these redundant benefits as having low priority leaves 36 cents of the premium dollar to pay net losses of victims.

But of those 36 cents, 21.5 cents go for something other than economic loss. The 21.5 cents are lumped together as "general damages" or "Pain and suffering" which, in the typical case today, are simply by-products of the bargaining process of insurance adjustment. Once we look beyond the name which the operators of the fault insurance system have given this non-economic portion of liability payments and understand what it really is in the usual case, it assumes a low priority by any social or humane standard.

That leaves just 14.5 cents out of the premium dollar as compensation for the net economic loss of the accident victim.

The numbers may have changed somewhat since 1970, but not a great deal. Why? Because the system has changed very little. The lawyers fight tooth and nail to preserve it.

Fairness: Pain And Suffering

Assuming no drastic changes in safety statistics, almost half of all drivers will be involved in one or more automobile accidents within the next four years. Three-fourths of those who drive will have an accident within the next seven years. All but one in a hundred will have at least one within the next twenty years.

Fortunately, most of these accidents will be trivial. But once an accident is set in motion, "luck" has a lot more to do with its severity than "fault." A drunk driving without headlights runs a red light and smashes into the passenger side of another vehicle in which no passenger happens to be riding. Later that day, a usually cautious motorist, spotting his spouse passing in the arms of another driver, momentarily loses his concentration, runs the same red light—and plows through an entire Cub Scout troop. Under the fault system, the first man—the drunk—would likely encounter no extraordinary hardship. His insurance company would pay for the damage he did and perhaps raise his rates or cancel his policy. The second man would see his life virtually ruined. His insurance would never be enough to pay all the claims, so it would protect neither him nor the children he had injured. It's all very well to be able to sue a driver under the fault system for $2 million. But if he's only got $20,000 of insurance and insignificant personal assets, $20,000 is all you are going to get (less legal fees).

So many people are involved in auto accidents each year one can only conclude that "even nice people" may, to their great regret, occasionally be at fault in the way they drive. It would be hard not to forgive all but the most reckless among them—for whom criminal penalties are, and should be, available. That being the case, and with luck rather than fault such a large determinant of how bad an accident actually turns out to be, the question becomes: How important is it—even when you can do it—to assign fault in auto accidents? Should society commit tens of thousands of its best minds to the task? Or are accidents not simply a hazard of whizzing around in 200 million registered motor vehicles?

Lawyers object that to compensate innocent victims only for their medical costs and lost wages, and not also for their pain and suffering, is unfair. Which is true. But life is unfair, and it is only a relative few serious accident victims who have the good fortune to have been injured by someone rich, or richly insured. The drivers with the least insurance cause the most accidents. And even if the offending party is well insured, there is the small matter of proving he was at fault. Years may pass. And then in all but a few cases it is questionable whether the injured party, after giving up a third or a half of his award in legal fees and expenses, retains more than would have been paid, promptly, under no-fault. (Remember, attorneys take a portion not just of the pain-and-suffering award, but of the award for medical expenses and lost wages, as well. In arriving at awards, juries are instructed to take no account of legal fees.)

Nor need no-fault necessarily exclude compensation for pain and suffering. At increased cost, a schedule of "pain and suffering" awards on top of economic damages could easily be added to a state's no-fault law if the citizenry so desired. (Or it could be offered as an option, at registration, or sold privately.) Rather than tie such a schedule to a multiple of medical expenses—which just gives victims an incentive to increase their medical expenses—there would be a small number of prescribed levels of pain-and-suffering compensation: Level 1, for a minor accident involving no broken bones or extensive medical treatment—no extra payment at all. Level II, for a relatively minor injury—$500 or $1,000. All the way up to Level V, say—$50,000 for a really tragic, permanent disability (with that money to be paid on top of actual economic damages, remember). The insurance adjuster would classify the accident by level; an appeals board could be established with authority to review policyholder challenges to those classifications. But the bulk of the award would be for economic damages, promptly paid, undiluted by legal fees. That being the case, the pain-and-suffering award would be relatively less important to both parties. At worst, one or the other might be believe the appeals board had misclassified the injury by one level.

And to keep the cost of no-fault low, such a system of modest benefits might itself be optional—perhaps an extra $100 at registration each year—so that only those who wanted the extra coverage would have to pay for it.

Who Opposes No-Fault

Insurers have ostensibly supported no-fault, but their support has not been vigorous. They've used it as a good way to deflect criticism from themselves, but few have really pushed hard for true no-fault. Their lawyers fear it, naturally, as it would put many of them out of work. Some companies fear, too, that no-fault, because it is so simple, would eventually lead to the same sort of group coverage as group life and health: employers would provide it as fringe benefit. That would be good for the firms that already specialize in group business, and good for the public at large, but a major blow to the insurers and 46,000 insurance agencies that exist to sell each policy separately. Not to mention the fact that, by shortening the time between accident and payment, an insurer also shortens the length of time it has to invest our premiums. Or that, by making auto insurance more efficient and less risky, no-fault would make it a smaller business, with fewer premium dollars to invest. So insurer support of no-fault has been widespread but shallow.*

Those who openly oppose no-fault—primarily America's small but powerful cadre of personal injury attorneys—take public opinion

---

*A particularly inane aspect of our existing no-fault laws are their subrogation requirements, under which one insurer goes after another for reimbursement of the money it's paid out. What could be more costly—and wasteful—than to have State Farm and Allstate arguing (behind the scenes) over whose driver was at fault and, accordingly, who should reimburse whom? Over and over, thousands and thousands of times each year. Yet that's how it works in many no-fault states.

surveys to show that the public doesn't want it. "Do you believe," they ask, "that the person who causes an accident, or his insurance company, should pay for the injuries he does to others?" Naturally, everyone answers yes. This is taken to show overwhelming grass-roots support for the traditional fault system of auto insurance.

Or they will cite the soaring costs of insurance in states that have adopted no-fault. But this is equally misleading. In the first place, auto insurance rates have been going up everywhere. Second, because most "no-fault" states have such a low threshold of damages beyond which the fault system takes over, drivers in those states are in effect paying for *both* systems.

Where fair comparisons have been done, by the U.S. Department of Transportation and others, they show—what else could they show?—that under no-fault payment is faster, fairer and more efficient. A higher proportion of the premium dollar is paid in benefits; and, of benefits, a higher proportion is paid for medical costs and wage loss, where it is most needed.*

Our failure to adopt true no-fault auto insurance is a nuts-and-bolts example of America at its most obese, arteries hardened and clogged by special interests, its heart having to pump $1 in liability premiums to get 14.5 cents where it is most needed—the economic losses of the accident victim. But what special interest group is better able to strangle the system than the lawyers? They write the laws.

Don't think of true no-fault as losing the right to sue. Think of it as gaining the right not to *be* sued. Think of it as revoking the lawyers' right to profit from your loss. And think of it as gaining the right to prompt, full payment of virtually all your actual medical costs and economic losses.

---

*The following exchange of letters, while more than 25 years old, illustrates the fault system at its worst.

From an Oregon claims adjuster to the claims manager in the Illinois home office: "Liability is most unfavorable. Our insured, as we previously advised, admits drinking. As a matter of fact, our insured indicates that he does not know just what happened as he came up the hill. . . We feel that we could put [the injured party] off for possibly six months through legal maneuvers, but finally a trial would take place. We feel the longer this can be put off without suit being brought, the more hungry they will get and the less they will demand."

Reply from the home-office claims manager months later (there may have been intervening correspondence, but the case was still dragging on): "Obviously, we will have no alternative but to [pay] the policy limits. . ... However, before you make the offer, kindly advise whether or not we would be liable for the plaintiff's attorneys' costs in the event suit is filed. If we are not, I would suggest you let the matter go to suit, and we can always settle on the courthouse steps."

QUESTIONS

47. You mean I couldn't sue Toyota for faulty brakes?
Suits against auto manufacturers (for faulty design) and local governments (for hazardous conditions) *would* still be allowed.

48. Wouldn't removing the threat of a lawsuit lessen the incentive to drive safely?
Even under no-fault, there's enormous incentive not to cause an accident. You could die; you could go to jail; you could lose your license; your own car could be wrecked; you could kill someone. True no-fault wouldn't make the reckless any more reckless. And charging for it at the pump would at least get them to pay a share of the cost instead of driving uninsured.

49. What if a guy purposely hits me?
This surely doesn't happen very often, but if someone chose to use his car as a weapon, to hit someone he knew (a creditor, perhaps? an in-law?), he would naturally be subject to criminal prosecution and civil lawsuits.

50. What about pedestrians?
A pedestrian injured by an automobile would be prevented from suing the driver, but automatically entitled to the all the benefits of PPN. If I hit a pedestrian, he would file a PPN claim with my insurer.

51. If I'm paralyzed for life because of some low-life, why *shouldn't* I have the right to sue?
This is really the heart of it, isn't it? Who *wouldn't* feel rage in a situation like this? But the reality is that most low-lifes have little to sue for, even if you win. And wealthy low-lifes will usually have enough insurance to protect them from any real pain. So retribution, to the extent it's possible or desirable, should probably come mainly through the criminal justice system. Perhaps reckless driving penalties should be stiffened. But that's beyond the scope of PPN. What PPN does is assure adequate reimbursement for your economic losses.

Anyone who wanted, in addition, a multi-million-dollar award to help compensate for his suffering—which unquestionably may be real and agonizing—would be free to buy extra coverage just as he might now buy extra travel and accident insurance.

Chapter 6

EMPOWERING THE CONSUMER
(The Report Card)

You have an accident, you file a claim. At the end, you get to give the insurance company a grade.

That's not how it works today, but that's how it would work under PPN. And the grades you give would really count.

On page 65 is a sample Customer Satisfaction Ballot that insurers would be required by law to provide all claimants at the conclusion of each claim. Unfortunately, this book is too small to reproduce a full-size sample. But it's not hard to picture. The ballot would be printed on a single, eight-and-a-half-by-eleven sheet of "card stock." The bottom third, below a perforation, would be the actual ballot—a business-reply postcard that you'd fill in and drop in the mail. It would be addressed to the state Insurance Department (or perhaps to a Big Six accounting firm, as described in Question #46).

On the front of the sheet, above the perforation, would be this letter:

Your opinion counts!

Dear Accident Victim:

By law, everyone who files an auto insurance claim must be given a Claim Satisfaction Ballot to grade the performance of his or her insurer. Your postage-paid ballot is at the bottom of this page. Just fill it out, tear it off at the perforation, and drop it in any mail box.

You are not required to send in this ballot, but we hope you will, because *your opinion counts.* Along with thousands of others, it will help determine how much business your insurer will be allowed to bid on next year. If you received a prompt, fair settlement, we want to give your insurer the chance to insure more drivers. But if your insurer earns below-average grades, we will reduce the number of drivers it may bid on serving.

This system will not guarantee that *every* claim is settled to every claimant's satisfaction. But it gives insurers a very real incentive to perform well for you, and it gives your opinion far more weight than in the past, when complaints were often ineffective or ignored.

Be assured that safeguards are in place to disallow submission of duplicate ballots; to prevent subversion of this process by insurers; and to interpret the results sensibly (for example, a severe accident is given more weight than a cracked windshield).

Please note that your insurer is required to provide this form with the top portion already filled out for you. If you believe it has been filled out incorrectly, make any corrections you wish.

Rutherford B. Hayes
Superintendent of Insurance

- - - - - - - - - - - - - - - - - -

Tear here and mail. No postage required.

Tear here and mail. No postage required.

_ _

CLAIM SATISFACTION BALLOT

INSURER: [*This comes pre-printed*]
CLAIM NUMBER: [*Filled in by insurer*]
DATE OF CLAIM: [*Filled in by insurer*]
NATURE OF CLAIM: [*Filled in by insurer*]
SETTLEMENT DATE: [*Filled in*]   **AMOUNT:** [*Filled in*]

NAME: [*Insurer fills in your name*]
VEHICLE REGISTRATION #: [*Insurer fills in*]

OVERALL, I WAS (check one):

[   ] COMPLETELY Satisfied
[   ] QUITE Satisfied
[   ] FAIRLY Satisfied
[   ] NOT TOO Satisfied
[   ] DISSATISFIED
[   ] HIGHLY DISSATISFIED

I'm dissatisfied because my settlement was (check all that apply):

[   ] Too slow *(it took ___ weeks)*
[   ] Too low *(I felt I deserved $_____ more)*
[   ] Handled without proper courtesy

DATE: _____   **SIGNATURE:** _____

(On the reverse of the letter there could be safety tips or more information about how PPN works and what the claimant had a right to expect from his insurer.)

The Ballot itself would be simple. And the top portion would be filled in by the insurance company *for* you—its name, the ID number and date of your claim, and so on. You'd only have to correct any of that you felt was in error, fill in your "grades," sign and mail.

But the computer program that did the tabulating could be fairly complex, both in terms of the "grading" it performed (e.g., weighting big claims more heavily than small ones), and in terms of the reports it could provide the Insurance Department.

In tabulating the forms, the computer would flag duplicate claim numbers and perform other checks. (One simple procedure—for a computer—would verify that the driver's vehicle registration number matched the insurer it had been assigned to.) In addition, spot checks could be done at audit-time to assure that bogus ballots had not been submitted. And claimants who were *not* supplied ballots would be encouraged to notify the Insurance Department—instances of that, too, would figure into an insurer's "grade."

The grading wouldn't be "perfect," but it would certainly make it possible to spot insurers who were performing significantly worse than average, as well as those doing better. Most insurers would wind up doing about average, and would suffer no penalty nor earn a reward. But any who scored worse than average would see their right to bid the following year shrink (or be revoked altogether, if the score were bad enough); any who scored above average would be rewarded with a shot at higher market-share.

The three best things about this system are:

1. **It empowers the consumer.** His vote counts.

2. **It provides insurers concrete incentive to satisfy claimants.**

3. **It protects nonclaimants.** Currently, you only know if you're dissatisfied with your insurer after it's too late! And even if you do then switch, that does nothing to help thousands of other poor saps in line for the same bad service. Under *this* system, there's a chance you'll be switched to a better carrier *before* you have a claim.

QUESTIONS

52. How do you keep the insurers from "stuffing the ballot box" with favorable fake ballots?

Each ballot has the claimant's name, vehicle registration and claim number. If the insurer submitted two ballots with the same numbers, the computer would catch it. If they invented phony claims, they would risk being caught in spot-check audits. I.e., the auditor would check to see whether the owner of the registered vehicle had ever filed such a claim. If the claim turned out to be bogus, the insurer would be guilty of fraud. (Naturally, a fair number of fake "good" ballots could be filed before anyone got caught. But to make a real difference in the score, an insurer would have to forge hundreds of ballots—and almost surely be caught.)

53. How do you keep insurers from "forgetting" to send ballots to people they know are angry?

This is a more legitimate concern. The first thing you would do is try to make everyone aware that this is what they're supposed to get when they have an accident—a Customer Satisfaction ballot. Chances are, by the time PPN got enacted, most drivers would have learned quite a bit about its basic features, and the Customer Satisfaction ballot is one of its *most* basic.

The second thing you would do is require the ballots to be sent automatically with the final check . . . and to have the department that disburses checks be responsible for enclosing the ballot. It would require quite a conspiracy to get the department selectively to avoid including ballots.

The third thing you might do is require winning insurers to print the following brief notice on *all* the auto insurance settlement checks it issues (including initial checks subject to the final settlement)—right on the back of the check itself, at the top, just above where the recipient will endorse it: "Note: If this check is in final settlement of an auto insurance claim, it MUST be accompanied by a business-reply Customer Satisfaction Ballot addressed to the State Insurance Department. If it is not, call 800-XXX-XXXX."

The type would have to be small, but that sure would make it hard for an insurer to get away with much.

Finally, it's important to note, most insurers don't *want* to get away with much. Unfashionable as it is to say it, most insurers, and insurance company employees, want to provide good service and fair settlements.

54. How do you keep insurers from just ripping up the unfavorable ballots?
They never get to touch the ballots. The ballots are mailed direct to the Insurance Department (or the tap-dancers at Price Waterhouse).

55. How do you "score" the ballots sensibly?
There's definitely an element of judgment in deciding how to weight the various factors. The Insurance Department would be wise to assign that job—in advance of enacting PPN—to a local consulting firm or perhaps to a faculty committee from the local university. But the broad outlines are fairly obvious. First, big claims would be given more weight than trivial ones. Second, dissatisfaction with the amount of the settlement should probably be weighted more heavily than dissatisfaction over speed or courtesy. Third, the degree of dissatisfaction over the amount should be proportional. Someone who got $13,000 in a settlement but thought it should have been $13,500 is obviously less of a concern than someone who got $200 and thought it should have been $700—even though, in both cases, the difference of opinion was $500.

But a fairly complex scoring formula, while it could take a thoughtful committee several weeks to work out initially, would be extremely easy to program, and for the computer to then compute.

56. How do you assure that people are fair and honest in their evaluations?
You don't! You'll surely have some nuts who say their $500 claim should have been settled for $5 billion, or simply people who received perfectly reasonable service but who, nonetheless felt they'd been stalled or treated rudely or short-changed.

The beauty of "the law of large numbers" is that, with blocks of 5,000 randomly selected vehicles, this is not a concern. One block of 5,000 vehicle owners is likely to contain almost exactly as many nuts and ne'er-contents as any other. It would be the *relative* score of one insurer compared with another that would matter.

57. You say a high-scoring company should be allowed to bid on more business. But what if it loses?
Good point. Rather than reflect customer satisfaction by increasing the amount of business a company could bid on, it might make

more sense to reflect it by adjusting the bids themselves. In other words (and the rules for this would be spelled out well in advance, so there would be no question who won which bid), if an insurer bid $2.5 million for a block of business, that bid could be adjusted to account for its Customer Satisfaction score. A bad score might penalize the bid by 3%—or a very bad score, by 10% or even more—meaning that the $2.5 million would be recorded, for the purposes of seeing who won the business, as $2.6 million or $2.8 million. Meanwhile, a company with a very good score might get a "credit"—not in actual dollars, but for the purposes of seeing who won the bidding. So that if a particularly good company also bid $2.5 million, it might be scored as if it had bid $2.3 million or $2.4 million (yet be paid the full $2.5 million if it won the bid).

Faced with two companies bidding almost the same amount, the "better" company would thus be rewarded with the business.

Any such credits and debits wouldn't be large; a small adjustment would be all that were required to steer business toward the best insurers. And the system of credits and debits would have to be established and made public at the outset of PPN (and never changed without plenty of warning, so changes couldn't be made after the fact to rig a particular outcome). But it may well be the best way to go.

Chapter 7

COLLISION and THEFT
(Yes and No)

The really big costs borne by auto insurance aren't smashed fenders but rather crushed vertebrae. Still, because only about 1 million of the nation's 11 million annual crashes involves any injury, many people think of auto insurance mainly as a way to get their cars repaired.

PPN would cover that, too, but with limitations.

Why PPN Should Cover Property Damage

It's perfectly plausible to envision PPN *without* property damage coverage. After all, a lot of people right now don't buy collision coverage—why "force" everyone to carry it automatically?

So perhaps the PPN your state legislature designs will only cover you for injury and not for damage to your car. You can be sure the insurance agents, once PPN becomes a real possibility, will lobby hard to have collision excluded so you at least have to buy *that* one policy at a time, through them. One can almost see the quiet agreements being made between the lobbyists and legislators (many of whom are insurance agents themselves, or lawyers who represent insurance companies).

Still, there are compelling reasons to include no-frills collision coverage as one of the benefits of PAY-AT-THE-PUMP, PRIVATE, NO-FAULT auto insurance, so long as it can be done in a way that's fair.

For one thing, everybody needs it. They may not need top-of-the-line coverage—and under PPN they wouldn't get it. But anyone who drives needs, at the very least, a car that will run. Whether or not it's paid for by insurance, almost anyone involved in a crash today fixes his car at least enough to be able to drive it again . . . and, in most cases, makes at least basic cosmetic repairs. So, as with liability insurance, why sell something one policy at a time that we know everybody needs?

A second reason to include collision is to keep things simple. Most people would find that PPN is all the coverage they need. So for most people, one of life's less pleasant little chores—worrying about auto insurance—would simply disappear. Like long division.

A third reason would be so that, in the event of a claim that involved injury as well as damage to your car, you wouldn't have to deal with two separate insurance companies. Not that this would be so awful—many of us pay state income tax separately from federal, and much of the job is handled simply by including a copy of one return with the other. But why bother? If we're fixing the auto insurance system, why not fix it right?

A fourth reason is that by removing the selling costs and by instituting certain other economies (read on), PPN would make collision coverage less expensive, and thus more affordable. What doesn't make sense for many people to buy now—or that they can't afford—*would* make sense under PPN.

Ironically, the people who today choose not to carry collision insurance are often the ones who need it most—they just can't afford it. Yes, a lot of well-to-do families sensibly choose not to insure their older vehicles for collision, because they can afford the risk of damage. But what is the lower-income person to do if *his* car becomes undriveable after an accident? Walk to work? The lower-income person often declines collision coverage not because he doesn't need it, but because, as it's now designed, he can't afford it.

What It Should Include

Today, collision coverage is unnecessarily expensive. Apart from the one-by-one selling costs, it encourages people to "over-repair" their cars. It's not *their* money, after all. Many demand "genuine" replacement parts (from Ford or GM or Honda), when competing parts—or even used or remanufactured parts—may be perfectly suitable and significantly less expensive. They demand expensive "good-as-new" cosmetic repairs, when "if it were their money" they might cut a few corners and save hundreds or even thousands of dollars.

Under PPN, the basic coverage would be for *functional* repairs—to return the car to full, safe driveable condition approximating the condition before the accident—and for "reasonable but not complete cosmetic repair."

The fine print could go into detail only auto experts understand. But the basic notion would be to allow the use of the least expensive parts suitable to the job, so long as they bore the name and guarantee of a legitimate manufacturer. And to get the car looking "decent," without necessarily looking "perfect." Dents would be banged out and repainted, but might still be noticeable (the color might not perfectly match). And so on. The repair standards wouldn't be shoddy or substandard; they would be appropriate and sensibly functional, with a strong emphasis on safety and reliability, relatively little emphasis on cosmetics.

Drivers would be free to pay extra to get "good-as-new" repairs. But the extra would come out of their own pocket. Either they could buy additional insurance privately to cover whatever PPN did not, or—better—they could simply pay at the time of the repair. The estimate for basic PPN repairs might be $800; but the repair shop might then eagerly give you a list of possible extras to consider. You want genuine Ford parts instead of the ones from Mitsubishi? That'll be an extra $280. You want a brand new fender instead of the decent-but-imperfect job our body shop can do? Great! An extra $450. And so on. Today, we effectively take "all" the extras if we're making a claim. Why not? They're free. Under PPN, we'd pick and choose only the ones we really think are worth the money.

How To Keep It Fair

To keep from subsidizing the Rolls Royce set, the deductible might be set at $250 or 5% of the Blue Book value of the car, whichever is more. Thus the owner of a car worth $7,000 would be covered beyond the first $350, while the Rolls Royce owner would have to foot the first $6,000 or so himself.

Additionally, there might be a $25,000 cap, because that would be enough to cover almost everyone. (Many cars that cost more initially are not worth more once they're driven out of the showroom.) Those who drive more valuable vehicles could either self-insure the difference, or buy additional coverage privately. (The difference might be a "scheduled item" on the driver's homeowner's policy, along with theft coverage—see below.)

The idea is by no means to penalize drivers of expensive cars; simply to provide a basic level of affordable, hassle-free insurance to the vast majority of drivers, while allowing the owners of high-cost vehicles to obtain complete coverage privately, but at extra cost—just as they do now.

There would also be a cap tied to 85% of the Blue Book value of the car.* This would help avoid sinking more into repairing a car than it's worth, and it would build in a margin of safety for PPN. In a total loss, people reimbursed for 85% of their car's value could either go out and buy an equally valuable car, covering the last 15% themselves, or they could buy something a little less expensive.

Obviously, there is nothing sacred about any of these numbers. But they are an example of a simple way to make the collision portion of PPN reasonably fair.

Expensive cars tend to cost more to repair than inexpensive ones—but that would even out, because of the 5%-of-Blue Book deductible. Yes, the owner of a $20,000 car would get far more from PPN if it were totaled than the owner of a $3,000 car. But the great majority of accidents are much less severe, and in that great majority of situations, it would be the owner of the $3,000 vehicle who would come out ahead. In little accidents, PPN would pay nothing to repair the expensive car, because the cost of repair would not exceed the deductible, whereas the fellow in the clunker would be reimbursed for anything above $250.

And there are other important ways to assure fairness. One obvious one is to collect all or part of the PPN collision premium at registration, as a small percentage of the Blue Book value of the car—say, 1%.

Another, as mentioned in Chapter 3, is to adjust the deductible based on where the accident actually occurs—for example, lower the deductible by 50% for accidents occurring in rural areas; raise it by 50% for accidents occurring in high risk zones. This is fairer to the

---

*The Blue Book, published by the National Automobile Dealers Association, comes in four different versions, three of which are orange. But then there's the Black Book (which is green), published by the National Auto Research Division of Hearst Media Corp. and widely used by dealers and insurance adjusters. PPN would use the guide that seems most closely to reflect the "retail" price of the car—the price you or I might pay to buy the same used car, in about the same condition. (The books give prices for good, average and poor condition vehicles, and suggest "normal" mileage ranges, outside of which adjustments should be made.)

city dweller who uses his or her car mostly to drive "out to the country" (why should he not get a break compared with the city dweller who drives mostly in town?)

Making It Optional

One reason to collect the collision portion of PPN at registration each year—apart from making it possible to tie the premium directly to vehicle value to make it fair—is to make it optional.

Although the PPN collision coverage just described would appear to offer a very good basic value, and would cost only a fraction of what most people pay for collision coverage now, some might prefer to opt out of it—either because they simply can't afford it, or because they want to purchase more complete coverage elsewhere.

That's OK.

With some kinds of group insurance, like group life insurance, the ability to "opt out" is dangerous, because you run the risk of having the "best risks" leave to buy cheaper coverage elsewhere. You're left with an ever riskier set of customers, which drives rates up—and causes even more good risks to defect.

That wouldn't be an issue with PPN collision coverage. To begin with, by offering bare bones coverage with no sales cost, it would be hard to imagine many people getting a significantly better deal if they shopped for it individually. How many people do you know who choose to drop out of the company health insurance plan, or wish that they could, in order to buy an individual policy? On top of that, when it comes to something like life insurance, only the insured is at issue: if he's young and healthy, chances are he won't die. But with auto insurance, good drivers are frequently involved in accidents. They don't *cause* as many, of course; but a smashed fender is a smashed fender no matter who caused it, so an insurer would have to charge even a great driver a fairly high premium, plus some minimum amount for the expense of signing him up.

If PPN collision coverage were optional, the auto registration renewal bill you got each year on a vehicle with a Blue Book value of $7,100 might look something like this:

```
┌─────────────────────────────────────────────────────────────┐
│                AUTO INSURANCE RENEWAL BILL                    │
│                                                               │
│        Please see the instructions on the reverse of this bill.│
│                                                               │
│  Your state auto registration fee:              $   25.00     │
│                                                               │
│  Insurance surcharge for high-risk vehicle      $____0.00     │
│                                                               │
│  Vanity License Plates ($35)                    $_____     │
│                                                               │
│  PPN Collision Coverage (XXX out if not desired) $__71.00     │
│                                                               │
│  Lost wages from $25,000-$50,000 ($100)         $_____     │
│                                                               │
│           from $50,000-$75,000 ($100)           $_____     │
│                                                               │
│              TOTAL PAYMENT ENCLOSED  $_____                │
└─────────────────────────────────────────────────────────────┘
```

The computer would know from the vehicle make, model and year what high-risk surcharge to apply, if any; and what the collision insurance premium should be (1% of Blue Book). For most vehicles, the collision premium would go down each year with the value of the car.

The instructions would explain all this, and explain the optional coverages. The form would be designed and the instructions written with the help of a local advertising agency skilled in communicating simply and effectively. Registrants would be cautioned to consider the extra disability coverage only if they earned substantially more than $25,000 a year. They'd be told just what the optional collision coverage provided in terms of "functional" repairs, and the importance of saving up to be able to cover the deductible portion themselves. They'd be urged to forgo the collision coverage only if they were certain they couldn't afford it or didn't need it.

(If someone did decline collision but later wanted to have it without having to wait until the following year's registration to sign up, there would be a $25 or $50 service charge for the administrative cost of handling his case manually and pro-rating the premium.)

The Importance Of The Deductible

Today, many people buy insurance they don't need—insurance to cover small losses they could cover more economically themselves—while failing to buy insurance they *do* need, to cover the really big losses that could wipe them out.

PPN helps solve this. It provides a great deal of needed coverage many people currently lack, but with a reasonably high deductible to keep them from having to pay for coverage that's uneconomical.

PPN's fairly high deductible helps to keep it affordable, which is important. And it also strikes a small blow for efficiency generally, which benefits us all: It eliminates millions of claims that would otherwise eat up countless hours in paperwork and hassle. You got a little dent? Fix it, don't fix it—but don't bother everybody about it!

Why spend $100 in administrative time and effort (including your own) arranging reimbursement for a $300 dent? That just makes it a $400 dent!

Over time, all but the unluckiest drivers will find that the money they save handling the little stuff themselves, instead of buying insurance to cover it, will greatly exceed what they would have gotten back from insurance benefits on these little claims. After all, insurance companies aren't handling small claims as a favor. Rather, and very reasonably, they attempt to build into your premium (on top of what it costs to actually fix your dent) all their expenses, all their overhead, all the fraudulent and padded claims they have to pay, plus a profit. You can avoid paying for all that. Just take a high deductible and pay to fix the dent yourself.

Another plus: When people are paying for something themselves, they tend to shop for it more carefully than when it's free. And when repair shops know you're paying the bill, not some huge faceless insurer, they tend to charge less and, sometimes, suggest less expensive alternatives.

And with a high deductible, there's less likelihood of fraud. Figuring you carry a $100 deductible, a mechanic may offer to render a $450 bill for a $350 repair, so you can get "full coverage." Hey, it's only fair after all you've paid in over the years. (It's *not* fair, it's fraud.) But if your car is worth $11,000, and thus your deductible is $550, it would be so much more clearly a fraud—pumping a $350 repair up to $900—that fewer people would be likely to do it.

Coping With The Deductible

All this is not to make light of the burden that a high-deductible can place on a family with little or no savings. An unexpected $600 expense (5% on a car with a Blue Book value of $12,000) is no fun for anybody. But there are three ways to protect against it (well, four if you count just buying a slightly less expensive car in the first place, so you have the $600 to begin with).

The first and most expensive way is to pay an insurer to protect you against it, by choosing a policy with a low deductible. Over the years, you'll pay in a lot more than you get out, so as to help pay for all the aforementioned overhead and fraud the insurer must contend with, plus its profit.

The second way is to wait for the accident to occur and then put the bill on your credit card. That saves having to pay insurer overhead and so forth, but saddles you with more high-interest credit card debt.

The third and by far the best way is to set up a "self-insurance" savings account designed (in your mind, at least, if not by the bank) for exactly this kind of rainy day. If you can build it to $1,500 or $2,000 or so, it may never run dry . . . and in the meantime, it's earning *you* a little interest.

Today's auto insurance system pushes people toward low deductibles. Agents compensated on commission make more money if you take a low deductible. And they also know that if and when you do call to report a claim, they'll enjoy the conversation more if they can tell you "all but $100 is covered" than if they have to remind you that they advised you to take a high deductible.

PPN would push people toward more economical deductibles. Those who did want just $100 deductible—who simply couldn't save for the inevitable dent or stolen stereo on their own—would doubtless be bombarded with offers of "PPN-gap" coverage, just as older folks are today bombarded by "medigap" offers. And they should naturally be free to buy it.

A Modest Proposal: Self-Insurance Accounts

To help people save for small emergencies—the $500 loss not covered by insurance—savings institutions and commercial banks should be allowed to offer "Self-Insurance Accounts." Really, they would be very much like any other savings account. Only, rather than returning just 40 or 50 or 60 cents of each dollar deposited, as insurance policies, on average, do—the rest going to sales costs, overhead, claims settlement costs, fraud and profit—Self-Insurance accounts would return the full dollar, plus interest.

The twist would be that to qualify for such an account, and a relatively high rate of interest, depositors would agree not to withdraw funds before, say, five years' time, *except to pay the uninsured portion of casualty losses.* If your car were hit and required $1,000 of repairs, only $500 of which was covered by insurance because of the deductible, you could without penalty withdraw $500 from your Self-Insurance Account. In the event of early withdrawal *other* than to pay for an uninsured loss, interest would be recalculated to a lower rate. This is the same system banks already use for "early withdrawal" from long-term savings certificates.

No doubt some depositors would lie about the reason for their withdrawals, presenting phony documentation of a loss in order to withdraw funds without penalty, but this would present no significant problem for the banks. The banks would not need to investigate or corroborate or "settle" depositors' claims, as insurers do, for they would only be giving back the depositors own money.

Banks could even offer the option of "billing" depositors a specified monthly or quarterly amount, to assist them in building their Self-Insurance Accounts. Or they could make automatic monthly transfers from checking and/or regular savings accounts.

For qualified depositors, the banks could also guarantee a predetermined emergency line of credit—$500 or $1,000 or more—in case the depositor suffered an uninsured loss *before* having saved up enough to pay for it.

Such mini-insurance accounts, would provide the man on the street with a much more economical way to protect against relatively minor losses. Instead of seeing much of his insurance dollar eaten up by insurance company costs, the full dollar—plus interest!—would all go to him. He would adjust his own claim. He would not have to pay for the fraudulent claims of others.

Of course, nothing prevents you from building a $1,000 or $2,000 emergency fund for this purpose right now. The advantage of the plan above is that it would provide discipline and incentive to help you do so. And the banks have the marketing clout to sell the idea. Not everyone is going to think of it on his own.

Why Theft Is Different

In big cities, according to the National Insurance Crime Bureau, the chance of your car being stolen this year is about 2%—one chance in 50. In Newark—the country's worst—it's about 5%. What's more, The NICB estimates that 15% of all stolen cars aren't really stolen at all—they're abandoned on purpose, or sold to chop shops for spare parts or sold abroad.

PPN could be designed to cover theft (and the other so-called "comprehensive" coverages, like fire). But because of the enormous incentive for fraud (need money? sell your car to a chop-shop and report it stolen), it may make more sense to leave theft coverages to the private market. And the private market could respond in several ways:

Auto insurers could of course sell theft policies, as now. But those same insurers offer homeowners insurance, and some might find it more efficient to offer the opportunity to list the family car as a "scheduled item," just as you can now schedule jewelry or art. (For a price, of course.)

Lenders could offer optional theft insurance just as they offer credit life. (The actual claims adjustment and investigative work could be subcontracted to auto insurers and others that specialize in claims adjustment.)

Auto makers could offer theft coverage efficiently, as well. Your dealer offers "extended warranties" and "financing"—why not theft insurance? If auto makers offered this option, it would give them an incentive to make their cars harder to steal. (Right now, it's good news in Detroit when a car is stolen by joy-riders and trashed—it means a new car has to be built.)

The more people competing for your business, the better.

Fighting Fraud

No task an auto insurer faces is more important—or difficult—than fighting fraud . . . from the petty, like the repair bill padded by $100, to the massive, like the "rings" of doctors and lawyers who have been caught manufacturing tens of millions of dollars in phony claims.

Studies suggest the insurance industry hasn't done a very good job of this—that a huge proportion of our auto insurance dollar goes to cover fraudulent claims. But neither do the studies suggest any easy ways to do better, given the current system.

PPN would reduce fraud significantly—by raising the deductible (eliminating lots of petty fraud) and by eliminating payments for pain-and-suffering (and thus much of the incentive to invent or "build" claims).

QUESTIONS

58. You mean I might have to deal with *two* insurance companies?
Well, most people wouldn't have to deal with even one. They'd have all the coverage they needed, automatically, and would only have to contact an insurance company if they had an accident whose cost exceeded the deductible.

But, yes, someone with two different vehicles would very likely be covered by two different insurers (depending on which blocks of business they were randomly assigned to, and which insurers won the bid for those blocks). And someone who bought extra coverage privately might wind up having to submit photocopies of his claim to the second company as well.

59. What if the 1% collision surcharge proves to be inadequate?
Insurance actuaries—especially after a year or two of experience with PPN—could figure out with considerable precision how high the registration surcharge should be. But getting it exactly right is not important. All that money would go into the overall PPN insurance pool; we'd simply have to be certain the overall pool was large enough to pay the insurers that won the right to handle our business. If, between them, the low bidders had won the right to insure the state's vehicles for a total of $2 billion, then the premium-at-the-pump, plus the various other fees would be set so that, combined, they'd rake in $2 billion a year, plus a little more as a margin for error.

In fact, we might consciously want to skew PPN collection away from registration (where it has to be paid in one less-affordable lump) and toward the gas pump (where it adds to people's incentive to drive efficiently).

60. If deductibles are tied to my car's value, why should I also have to pay a higher collision surcharge at registration?
Good question—and in some ways the same question as the previous one. We could handle the "fairness" issue for collision coverage pretty well with *either* the deductible or the surcharge at registration. Or, we could handle it with come combination of both.

Varying the deductible by vehicle value is attractive because it works so well to discourage small claims. If you simply made it a flat $250, it would be lower than is sensible for many people. Yet if you made it a flat $1,000—a risk any vehicle-owner with $5,000 or

$10,000 in savings could certainly bear—it would be a terrible burden on low-income people.

The fairness issue could probably solved quite well by varying the deductible amount alone. But it would still seem odd for the owner of a $35,000 vehicle not to be paying more for his collision coverage (notwithstanding the fact that, because of the deductible, he'd actually be getting less coverage) than the owner of a $1,500 vehicle. Justifiably or not, the owner of the $1,500 vehicle might feel better about PPN knowing that his collision surcharge is just $15, while the guy in the BMW is paying $350.

So a combination of the two "fairness" adjustments probably makes the most sense.

61. How would PPN collision coverage save money?

✓ By covering everyone automatically, you eliminate the sales and marketing costs, and the cost of trying to figure out how much each person, individually, should be charged.

✓ By setting high deductibles, you cut out millions of small claims that, proportionally, cost the most to administer. And you eliminate a great deal of petty fraud.

✓ By setting a standard of "functional" rather than "good-as-new" cosmetic repair, and allowing the use of competitive replacement parts, you greatly decrease the cost of claims, yet deliver the essential coverage everyone needs.

Chapter 8

CONS
(The Arguments *Against* PPN)

Most people like the notion of PAY-AT-THE-PUMP, PRIVATE, NO-FAULT auto insurance. Lawyers and insurance agents have a more complex reaction. Lawyers like the pay-at-the-pump part, but decry no-fault. Agents cheer for no-fault, but deride pay-at-the-pump.

It's a matter of simple self-interest: The 65,000 members of the Association of Trial Lawyers of America (ATLA) stand to lose billions of dollars in annual income—*personally*—if we cut them out of the system. So do the insurance agents. Much as they protest they're just looking out for our best interests, it's hard to believe they're able to gauge objectively what's best for us when so much of their own livelihood is at stake.

And lawyers and insurance agents aren't the only ones who will oppose PPN.

Oil companies and service station owners will oppose PPN, because it gives people an incentive to drive a little more efficiently and use a little less gas. What's good for the environment and our balance of trade deficit is bad for their profits.

Auto dealers may like the fact that PPN makes buying insurance—and thus a car—easier. But they won't like PPN's functional standard of repairs, because expensive repairs mean more profit to the dealer.

Insurance companies themselves are another matter. Most support no-fault insurance, at least half-heartedly. But most would also be loath to antagonize or alarm their agents and marketing staffs by advocating pay-at-the-pump—even if, in the long run, it would make them more money. And it *would* make more money for the most efficient insurers, who would be most likely to see their market shares expand in the competitive bidding.

One imagines those efficient companies might also breathe a sigh of relief if they were freed up to run their businesses with less regulatory oversight over rates (under PPN, they'd be free to make all the profit they could); and with less public animosity (in states like California and New Jersey, it's hard to imagine public opinion becoming any more hostile).

One imagines, too, that many insurers would prefer a less adversarial system, where they mainly worked with claimants to pay their legitimate claims, rather than fighting attorneys every step of the way. They would still have to be firm about costs and wary of fraud—claims settlement is not all sunshine and light—but much of the friction would be gone.

Still, not all insurance companies *are* efficient, and few are known as aggressive innovators or agents of change, so many are likely to resist PPN. But it could hardly be more energetic resistance than the industry put up to defeat California's Proposition 103—and they lost.*

NICO's Press Conference

In May, 1992, the National Insurance Consumer Organization called a press conference to announce its support of PAY-AT-THE-PUMP, PRIVATE, NO-FAULT auto insurance. NICO is headed by Robert J. Hunter, an insurance actuary who served as Federal Insurance Administrator under presidents Ford and Carter.

"The key problem regarding [PPN]," said Hunter in the report NICO distributed at the press conference, "is simply overcoming the likely huge opposition to the plan from those who have a vested interest in today's inefficient system. These entities will fight this plan very hard. They will point to gas price increases never mentioning the [overall] savings that people will enjoy. They will use the 'T' word (Tax), even though this will not be a tax but the same insurance premium we now pay, only collected and disbursed without their getting to grab a piece of it. They will say this is

---

*Prop 103, which passed by a margin of 51% to 49% in 1988, mandated, among other things, a 20% rollback in auto insurance rates. By the fall of 1992, nearly $200 million had been rebated to consumers (about $10 per car), with hundreds of millions more tied up in the courts. But Prop 103, while it had some good points, did relatively little to fundamentally overhaul our archaic system. In order to really fix auto insurance, you've got to slash *costs*, not just mandate lower prices.

government insurance, even though government merely assists in efficient premium collection and group formation. They will say this is a 'public,' socialist program when, in fact, it is a private free-market program.

"We are not naive regarding this opposition. It will be fierce and well-funded. But, insurers spent $70 million against Proposition 103 vs. $2 million by Ralph Nader's group and the insurers lost! The public is smart."

The insurance industry was quick to respond.

From *Best's Insurance Management Reports*, May 26, 1992:

> While the NICO plan may sound like the ideal consumer solution to many problems, it ignores many important issues, says Marc H. Rosenberg, VP of federal affairs for the Insurance Information Institute.
>
> "The insurance industry feels they've got it half right," Mr. Rosenberg said in a prepared statement. "Meaningful no-fault is an important reform which insurers have supported consistently over the years. Insurers welcome public advocacy of this needed reform by Mr. Hunter and Mr. Tobias."
>
> But that is the only good thing about the plan, he said. "For example, auto insurance costs more in urban areas because of greater frequency of accidents, higher rates of car theft and vandalism, etc. Yet motorists in rural and suburban areas—where greater distances are driven—would end up paying more for insurance because they use more gasoline per capita than do most urban drivers," Mr. Rosenberg said. "So rural and long-distance drivers would end up subsidizing urban drivers." *[No they wouldn't—see page 26. And remember, it was for exactly this reason theft would not be included in PPN.]*
>
> He also noted that while many owners of large sedans that get low mileage are considered safer drivers, they would end up paying more than those with small sports cars that get great gas mileage but historically cost more to insure. "Under the pay-at-the-pump plan, drivers of family cars would end up subsidizing drivers of sports cars," Mr. Rosenberg said. *[No they wouldn't—see page 25.]*
>
> He also criticized the various fees paid to register an automobile and the surcharges placed on tickets. "By the time they are finished enumerating these various modifications to what started out like a simple idea, one is left wondering how much benefit will be derived from substituting government bureaucracy and surcharges for private sector underwriting," Mr. Rosenberg said. *[No government bureaucracy would be required; there'd just be some tinkering with the computer program that calculates your auto registration fee, and tickets would cost more.]*
>
> "And when they are finished, NICO says, many consumers will be

shopping for private insurance!" *["Many" is misleading. Of America's 167 million drivers, a few million might choose to buy even more personal-injury and collision coverage than PPN provides. But what's wrong with that? And what's wrong with private insurance? PPN is private insurance, just as group health insurance is.]*

He noted that the pay-at-the-pump idea has been around for some time and said the biggest difference between old ideas and this latest plan is that the insurance premium per gallon estimate jumped from 25 cents a year ago to more than 50 cents today. "There is no reason to assume that this estimate will not rise again before the debate ends," he said.

[Oh, horse feathers. Estimates of the premium-per-gallon vary because different plans call for different levels of coverage. No one ever said 25 cents per gallon would be enough to provide full benefits of the type described in this book. But anything less than the 85 cents or so we now pay on average would be a net gain—especially because for most people the coverage PPN provides would be so much more complete. In any event, the price per gallon would not be set by regulators or by NICO, but by the free market. It would depend on the competitive bids of the insurance industry. Unless the Insurance Information Institute believes the industry would conspire to rig the bidding, it should not attempt to frighten people into thinking PPN would turn into some open-ended government boondoggle.]

Common sense tells you that PPN *must* be a better deal than the current system, because:

1. It is group insurance, with groups of 5,000 drivers each. Everyone knows group insurance is cheaper than individual insurance. Do you know *anyone* who wishes his employer didn't have a group health plan?

2. PPN eliminates the entire selling and billing process and eliminates the need to issue policies on each of the nation's 200 million registered vehicles.

3. PPN eliminates the lawyers. Is there *anyone* who thinks they do not jack up the cost of auto insurance?

4. PPN eliminates duplicate medical payments.

5. PPN eliminates pain and suffering "lottery" payments that go to a very, very few, yet jack up insurance rates for all.

(Anyone wishing to buy such extra coverage would be welcome to; but most of us would be thrilled simply to be assured full, hassle-free basic coverage.)

6. PPN eliminates the incentive to "build" medical expenses and lost wages, which under the current system are frequently multiplied threefold in determining settlement (which is then split with the attorney).

7. PPN reduces the smallest, least efficient claims by setting sensible deductibles and encouraging people to cover the relatively trivial risks themselves.

8. PPN sets a standard of decent, practical, functional repair, leaving those who desire "good-as-new" cosmetics free to pay the added cost themselves (or insure privately for the difference).

How much would all this save? It's hard to say with precision, but somewhere between "an awful lot" and "a tremendous amount." It would be a shame to be deflected from those savings simply because no one can put a precise number on them in advance.

And precisely what would the per-gallon premium be? The precise answer would depend on the precise benefits of the plan and the competitive bids insurers made to provide those benefits. But unless group insurance is *less* efficient than individual insurance, and unless lawsuits are *less* expensive than no-fault settlements, and unless duplicate medical payments somehow *save* money, the answer is that most of us would pay less than we're paying now. A good estimate, though, is around 40 cents a gallon, plus the surcharges at registration and ticketing.

(Because of the uncertainty the first year or two, insurers might bid high, which could mean a somewhat higher premium at first. Or conceivably they might bid low, to stake out market share, which could mean a lower premium at first. But in the long run, they'd learn what it costs to insure a block of 5,000 drivers, and bid just high enough to cover their costs and make a good profit—but not so high as to lose the bid. That's what competitive bidding is all about.)

The main thing opponents of PPN will try to do, as III's Rosenberg did, is "divide and conquer." Get the rural people fighting with the urban people, get the big-car people fighting with the small car people, and hope that none of them notice that—whatever the inequities—PPN would be a better deal for almost all of them!

No group insurance plan is entirely fair—witness group health plans where everyone, young, old, hale and frail, all pay the same rate. But is group insurance a bad thing?

And how fair is the auto insurance system *now?*

The bottom line is that PPN would be at least as fair as the current system—and vastly more beneficial.

The bottom line is that what's really unfair is how much of our money goes—unnecessarily—to things other than paying legitimate claims.

It's a debate that will never be "won." The lawyers and insurance salespeople who stand to lose billions will never say, "Oh, *now* I understand! Let's do it!" (A few actually do say that, but very few.) So the argument goes round and round, endlessly (as this chapter could)—and as long as it does, the lawyers and agents have just what they want: the status quo.

It's time to begin ending the debate and start fixing the system.

QUESTIONS

62. Are you saying that lawyers and insurance agents are, somehow, bad people? My brother's a lawyer!

So's mine. No, the people who oppose PPN are, for the most part, every bit as wonderful as anyone else. (And my brother, not being a *personal-injury lawyer,* favors no-fault. Many lawyers do.) This isn't a matter of good versus evil. It's a matter of self-interest. But if you doubt that fine, bright people, can put self-interest first, just look at all the fine, bright tobacco executives who tell us—to this day!—that there's no proof smoking is a health hazard . . . who insist the Joe Camel cartoon character (whom one study found to be as familiar to six-year-olds as Mickey Mouse) is not designed to appeal to kids. Self-interest is powerful stuff.

THEMES PPN OPPONENTS WILL STRESS

with a quick answer for each:

It's too complex.
Not for car-owners it isn't! They don't have to do *anything*. Just buy gas and renew their auto registrations. What could be simpler?

It's unfair.
Less so than now.

It's expensive.
We pay the equivalent of 85 cents a gallon for our insurance now, on average. PPN would cost significantly less, yet provide far more coverage than most people carry now.

It's regressive.
To the contrary. Today, those least able to afford auto insurance – the young and the poor – are most often charged the highest rate, even if they have spotless driving records. *That's* regressive.

It's ...
Hey! Just look at the big picture. PPN would cost most people less than now, but provide much better coverage. Why are you trying so hard to scuttle this?

Chapter 9

NEXT STEPS
(Making It Happen)

What's hard is not knowing what to do about auto insurance, but getting it done.

- [ ] How do you match the power of the trial attorneys and the insurance agents?
- [ ] How do you phase PPN in gradually to give people time to adjust?

You match the power of the trial attorneys and the insurance agents, it seems to me, by getting enough voters to understand how much better the system could be. It's naive to think change is easy, but cynical—and ultimately wrong—to think change is impossible.

And there are a couple of ways to phase it in.

The most important and obvious is simply to go one state at a time. The early states to adopt PAY-AT-THE-PUMP, PRIVATE, NO-FAULT would presumably be those like California, where dissatisfaction with the current system is greatest—and that have a "referendum" mechanism that allows measures to by-pass our elected representatives—and those like Hawaii, California and Florida, among others, where cross-border problems would be manageable.

In any given state, moreover, it might be possible to phase PPN in. For example, the cost and benefits might be phased in over five years, as outlined in the table below. I have not attempted to make the numbers actuarially sound, merely to illustrate the concept:

YEAR	Cents/ Gallon	Lawsuit Threshold	Collision Deductible
1	8 ¢	5,000	$ 4,000 or 30% of Blue Book
2	16 ¢	10,000	2,500 or 20% of Blue Book
3	24 ¢	15,000	1,500 or 15% of Blue Book
4	32 ¢	25,000	1,000 or 10% of Blue Book
5	40 ¢	no suits permitted	250 or 5% of Blue Book

In the first year, benefits for medical expenses and lost wages would be capped at $5,000 and lawsuits would be allowed for any additional damage. Collision coverage would be provided with a gigantic deductible. No one would abandon the current system. There'd still be tons of money for agents and lawyers.

But the handwriting would be on the wall, as each year the benefits were slated to rise until, in the fifth year, they would equal those described in this book. At that point, most people would have far more coverage than they do now, and no need for either agents or lawyers.

The problem with this concept is that it would require a lot of thinking on the part of insurers, trying to decide what to bid for blocks of business each year, and customers, trying to understand what their coverage was and what further coverage they needed.

It's too complex—and it would also give PPN opponents five years to find ways to subvert the process and return auto insurance to the status quo.

It would also be a rotten system in the first two or three years, because it would encourage people to "build" their medical expenses and lost wages to the threshold beyond which they could sue for damages.

It might simply be better to enact PPN—but with a two-three year delay until it actually took effect. That would give the state Insurance Department and everyone else plenty of time to work out the details, and give insurers and agents and lawyers time to adapt. (Would that the average Jane or Joe had so much notice of an impending lay-off!)

Another way to phase PPN in would be to separate its two sides. The pure-no-fault side is easily separated from the pay-at-the-pump side. It makes sense to do both—and to enact both at the same time, while public attention is focused on the issue—but that doesn't mean both must go into effect at once. True no-fault could go into effect first, with pay-at-the-pump to be phased in after a couple of years.

You could even make the no-fault side voluntary. Under this scheme, you would pass a law giving drivers a choice: They could give up their right to sue for pain and suffering (and their right to receive duplicate reimbursements) in return for a fat reduction in their premium. Or they could stick with the current costly system—and pay for it.

Most people, given the chance to cut their premiums significantly, yet retain the most important aspects of their coverage, would probably do so.

This is the brainchild of Professor Jeffrey O'Connell, known to many as "the father of no-fault" auto insurance. As he has pointed out: It's one thing for lawyers to fight laws that would *impose* true no-fault. But how can they argue against giving people the choice?

(For this to work, the standard auto insurance contract would be rewritten such that, in the event of a crash involving a claim for pain and suffering, the *claimant's* insurer would be the one liable for that extra payment. That way, insurers would know, in advance, what their risks were. Otherwise, one insurer might sign up everyone at the lower premium—only to find that all its drivers were crashing into drivers who had retained the right to sue.)

So there may be ways to phase in a good system. But it would be a mistake to let the lawyers and insurance agents make us work too hard to accommodate their needs.

We deserve a good, clean, logical, efficient auto insurance system. After all: we're the ones paying the bill.

QUESTIONS

63. What Can *I* Do?
Three things:
- ☐ Tear out one of the two letters to your governor in Appendix C and mail it in!
- ☐ Send NICO the coupon at the end of this book so you can be reached in case a drive for PPN gets going in your state.
- ☐ Give copies of this book to a handful of friends and colleagues. Spread the word. If you do, and they do, we'll succeed.

Appendix A:

WHAT TO DO IN THE MEANTIME

PPN won't be enacted overnight. Here are some thoughts on what to do in the meantime:

Shop Around

☐ *If you're rich,* just call your friendly insurance agent. He or she will know what to do. Why bother trying to get the best deal?

☐ *If you're not rich,* shop around! Prices for auto insurance vary tremendously. It's fine to get a price from your friendly independent insurance agent, and from **State Farm** (check your phone book), which has its own captive agents. If the price is as good as you could get elsewhere, or not much more, you may well want the personal touch. But call at least one or two "direct writers"—such as **GEICO** (800-841-3000) and **Worldwide Insurance** (800-325-1487)—for competitive quotes.

☐ *If you live in California,* be sure to call **20th Century Insurance** (818-704-3700). If you qualify—only preferred risks are accepted—you could cut your current insurance premiums in half.

☐ *If you live in New Jersey,* call **New Jersey Manufacturers**. Their rates and service are good, but you can also expect to get a good chunk of your premium *back* each year, when the company knows just how well or poorly it's fared.

☐ *If you know someone insured by AMICA insurance,* see if you can get him to recommend you. (AMICA won't even listen to you if you're calling them cold.)

☐ *If you are or were an officer in the Armed Forces,* call **USAA** (800-531-8080). They have terrific rates and very satisfied customers.

☐ *If you're over 50,* and thus eligible to join the American Association of Retired Persons, or already a member, call **AARP,** whose plan is administered by the Hartford Insurance Company (800-541-3717). They won't give a quote over the phone—they send an application that can take several weeks to process. But it could be worth it. "I cut my premiums in half when I went from Allstate to AARP," writes a friend from Illinois. In 1992, he was paying just $280 for good coverage on his 1989 Oldsmobile Delta 88.

☐ *If you're considered a poor risk* for some reason, but actually you're not—or you've turned over a new leaf—call the **Progressive Insurance Group** (800-283-1101), which has made a fortune learning to tell which seemingly bad risks aren't really so bad after all.

☐ *If you're considered a poor risk, and actually you are,* ask your GM, Ford or Chrysler dealer for help. Each has its own insurance subsidiary, in part to make sure customers can secure the coverage they need to get a loan.

Ask Your Mechanic

Once you narrow it down to one or two choices, you might want to call your local body shop and ask how those companies are about settling claims. If one is a pleasure to deal with and the other's a nightmare, buy your insurance from the first (and consider investing in the second).

Choose The Highest Deductible You Can Comfortably Afford

Paying someone to take risks you could afford to take yourself is *paying for something you don't need*—like paying for premium cable TV channels if you never watch them. True, after any given accident you may wish you had not saved money this way. But over a lifetime, unless you're a particularly poor or unlucky driver, you'll come out way ahead by self-insuring the small stuff. Remember: they're not offering this coverage for free. They expect to cover all their overhead, pay all the fraudulent claims, and so forth, and still make a profit. If you self-insure, you don't have to pay for the overhead or fraud, and you make your own profit.

On top of that, when damage is minor, it's often best not to file a claim at all, lest your insurance rates rise. So why pay for something you won't use?

Bonus: if you self-insure the small stuff, you save the hassle of filing the claim, submitting estimates, and so on.

For thoughts on setting up your own "self-insurance account," see page 78.

Consider Skipping Some Coverages Altogether

The highest deductible of all, of course, is not to buy collision or comprehensive coverage at all. This makes sense for owners of older cars with low resale values. Also for owners of expensive new cars—if they're very wealthy. Why does Ross Perot need to pay someone to protect him from the risk his car will be stolen?

Ask For A Discount

Many auto insurers offer discounts—if you ask. Often it's the highest-price companies that offer the most discounts, so you have to keep your eye on the bottom line. But if you qualify for a discount, you should certainly be getting it.

Your insurer may offer discounts for:

❑ Non-smokers
❑ Non-drinkers
❑ Graduates of drivers-ed programs
❑ Teenagers with good grades
❑ Families whose youthful drivers go away to school (leaving the insured vehicle safely behind)
❑ Families in which the only driver is a woman aged 30 to 64
❑ Vehicles driven less than 7,500 miles a year
❑ Vehicles equipped with air bags, automatic safety belts or anti-theft devices
❑ Drivers who carpool

❏ Drivers who insure two or more vehicles with the same company (you'll typically save about 15% by doing this)

❏ Drivers who haven't caused an accident in the past few years

At State Farm, in many states, drivers earn a 5% discount after three years' unblemished record, 10% after six years. Drivers who have had, within the past three years, an accident for which the company paid out $400 or more and for which the driver was 50% or more at fault, are charged 10% extra. Two such accidents, 30% extra. An adult male suburban Chicago resident who drove a 1992 Oldsmobile Cutlass sedan for pleasure only, and who carried a typical package of coverages, paid a basic premium of $540.96 a year. But it could run from as low as $497.40 (had he been accident-free for six years) to as high as $888.72 (if he had had three or more accidents). *If* State Farm chose to renew the policy at all.

Consolidate Your Business

It often makes sense to insure your home and your vehicles with the same company. You'll get a better rate, and be looked on more favorably if you should ever have to make a claim.

Buy Used Cars

As everyone knows, the minute you drive a new car off the lot it loses thousands of dollars in value. To many people, the excitement (and smell) of a new car is worth those thousands. But financially, if not olfactorily, it's smarter to buy a good used car—one reason being that you'll have less to insure, and, thus, lower insurance costs. (Also, of course: lower financing costs.) Someone who regularly buys used cars instead of new ones will save tens of thousands of dollars over his or her lifetime. Literally! If you do this, you may be looked down upon by your friends. But only until they need to come to you to borrow money. (Then they'll just hate you.)

Or At Least Cars That Aren't Expensive To Insure

Whatever kind of car you buy, it's worth a call to your insurance agent or direct writer to find out what it will cost to insure. If the muscle model is worth an extra $500 or $1,000 a year to you, fine. But if economy is on your mind, don't accidentally buy a car that's on insurers' "frequently stolen," "easily damaged," "expensive-to-repair," or "favored by reckless drivers" lists. As financial planner Jonathan Pond suggests: "Buy a frumpy car that the average thief would be embarrassed to steal."

Drive Defensively

You'll save a fortune on insurance if you have a clean driving record and no accidents. It's not enough just to drive lawfully (i.e., less than 10 miles an hour over the speed limit, as best I can figure it). Involvement in an accident even if you were blameless is often a strike against you when your rates are being determined.

Plus, driving defensively can keep you from getting killed.

Take A Course, Get A Discount

Some states require insurers to give a discount for those who have completed a Defensive Driving course administered by the National Safety Council.

Reports one Delaware driver who's taken the course both there and in New York (and whose view may be a little on the harsh side):

> For approximately $20 you get to sit through two evenings of what I'd call Driver's Ed for Idiots. In essence, it is a few hours of such obscure information as:
>
> ☐ Don't Speed
> ☐ Don't Drink and Drive
> ☐ Check Your Blind Spots
> ☐ Stay Out of Others' Blind Spots.
>
> You get the picture. But going through this torture gives me a 10% discount on my liability and Personal Injury Protection for three years. Since I've also taken the advanced course (a single three-hour session), the discount gets bumped to 15%. You can only take the advanced course when the first three-year period is close to expiring.

The Defensive Driving course saves him hundreds of dollars for a few hours work. Check with your insurer to see if there's a discount available, and for help finding the course. (You can also call the National Safety Council at 800-621-6244 to find the nearest course.)

If You Have An Accident

Take your time. Summon the police to file a report. Get the license and insurance information on the other driver, and the names, addresses and phone numbers of as many witnesses as possible—especially if you didn't cause the accident. Write down everything you can remember about the accident while it's fresh in mind. *Call your insurance company, or your agent, right away.* And, perhaps most important of all, start a file for all the paperwork that will accumulate. Don't throw anything out. Make brief but clear notes of all your contacts with the insurance company, body shop, health care providers, lawyers, and anyone else involved—and toss them in the file. (Or just start with a fresh yellow pad, and watch it fill up with notes as time goes on.) With luck, you won't need any of this. But it would be foolish not to have it.

If You Suspect Fraud

Here's a handy number to call if somebody at a party is bragging about how he ripped off his insurance company, or if you have reason to think he did: **800-TEL-NICB**. It's the National Insurance Crime Bureau's fraud hotline.

Obviously, you're not going to rat on a friend or relative (at least not a relative on your side of the family). But insurance fraud is a crime like any other, so if you'd call the police if you saw this guy stealing a car, you should probably call someone if you see him stealing from the insurance pool.

Making Sense Of The Coverages

In buying automobile insurance under the current system, you are buying several separate coverages:

Bodily injury (BI) is the most important. It protects you if you—or anyone else driving your car with your permission—injure pedestrians, people in other cars, or guests in your own car. It also covers you, and family members living with you, if you or they have an accident while driving someone else's car. Bodily injury coverage provides for your legal defense in the event of a lawsuit, and for payment of whatever settlement is made—up to the limits of the policy.

Property damage (PD) liability insurance works just the same way, only it covers damage to other people's *property.*

Liability coverages are typically expressed in a string of three numbers. If you select "10/20/5" coverage, then you're covered up to $10,000 for any person you damage, up to $20,000 for the whole lot of them (even if you've injured eleven); and up to $5,000 for damage to their property. (And you are woefully underinsured! Even "100/300" bodily injury coverage may not be enough to shield you from liability in a serious accident.)

Collision coverage pays you, regardless of fault, for damage to your car if it should hit something (other than a bird or animal) or turn over. It is limited to the value of your car at the time of the accident.

If you suffer property damage in a collision that was not your fault, you have a choice. Say you have $500 deductible collision coverage. You may collect from your own insurance company (which may then go after the other driver's insurance company for the full value of your loss and, if successful, return the $500 it deducted from your loss). Or you may file a claim for the full loss directly with the other driver's insurance company, which, if it agreed its policyholder was at fault, would pay your loss out of the policyholder's property-damage coverage. Naturally, your insurer would prefer you did the latter.

Comprehensive coverage reimburses you in the event of fire or theft, "glass breakage, falling objects, missiles, explosion, earthquake, windstorm, hail, water, flood, vandalism or malicious mischief, riot or civil commotion, or collision with a bird or animal." You may also be entitled to payment for personal belongings that were in the car, and for reimbursement for a rental car for a limited period of time.

Medical payments coverage pays medical expenses that you, and all members of your family living with you, may incur, whether riding in your own car or in someone else's, or if hit by a car. It also covers guests riding in your car or in some other car you are driving with the owner's permission. Typical limits are $1,000 or $5,000 per person. *If your family already has good medical insurance, you can save money by skipping this coverage.*

Uninsured motorist coverage protects you and family members living with you (and guests riding in your car) if injured through the fault of an uninsured or hit-and-run driver, or one whose insurance company goes broke before settling your claim. If it wasn't the other party's fault, you don't collect.

Personal injury protection (PIP) is offered or required in no-fault states. Depending on the state, it may provide just a few thousand dollars of coverage up to (in Michigan) unlimited medical expenses and certain other benefits. But because you can still be sued under these so-called no-fault laws for injury you do to others, if it meets an often-low "threshold" of severity, you will still need liability coverage.

Auto Rental Insurance

Only a good buy when the roads are incredibly icy, or if, even in good weather, you average about three accidents a year. Otherwise, forget it. You are automatically covered against major loss when you rent a car or truck; it is the small loss they are trying to get you to insure against. And that may already be covered under your existing auto insurance policy—or even by the credit card to which you charged the rental.

Umbrella Insurance

Anyone with appreciable assets to protect should have at least a $1 million personal liability policy. Any insurance agent can obtain this coverage for you, and it shouldn't cost much more than $150-$250 or so, even if you have more than one home or car. An umbrella policy picks up where your automobile and homeowners policies leave off (assuming you carry the standard maximum liability coverages). If we ever get true no-fault, you won't need this for your car (and the prices should drop even lower). But you'll still want to carry it in case some young rock star should come bounding up the stairs to shake your hand (perhaps mistaking you for someone else), only to slip and dislocate his vocal chords. Or you acidentally poison all the guests at your dinner party.

Toll-Free Help

For questions on *any* general insurance subject—auto, but also homeowners, umbrella, flood, life, health or any other kind—call 800-942-4242, the National Information Consumer Helpline (weekdays from eight to eight, Eastern time). It is run by the insurance industry, so the advice you get will obviously reflect the industry's point of view. But the industry knows a lot about insurance.

TIPS FROM THE NATIONAL SAFETY COUNCIL

The National Safety Council knows about accidents. You want to know how many people hurt themselves bowling last year? Four times more than hurt themselves boxing—22,515 (though one presumes the injuries were less severe). You want to know your chances of being struck and killed by lightning? About one in two and a half million (reason enough never to venture outdoors in June, July or August, when two-thirds of the deaths occur).

Here, then, are facts, tips, and myth-understandings from the National Safety Council:

Air Bags

By 1996, air bags will be standard in 90% of all new U.S. passenger cars, domestic and imported. They're designed to supplement the use of safety belts, not replace them—you're nuts not to buckle up. Here's how they work.

When a violent frontal impact occurs (but not an impact from the side or rear), sensors cause a solid chemical propellant sealed inside the bag to undergo a rapid chemical reaction. The propellant (principally sodium azide) turns mostly into nitrogen gas (the same gas that makes up 80% of the air we breathe). The gas inflates a woven nylon bag packed inside the steering wheel hub and the passenger-side dash board of bag-equipped cars. The bag inflates in less than a twentieth of a second, and the nitrogen is then vented through openings in the back of the bag.

The 'smoke' and 'residue' produced during the deployment of an air bag consist of corn starch and talcum powder which are used to lubricate the bag. Some components within the bag module, as well as the steering wheel hub, will remain hot for about 15 minutes after deployment—but should pose no threat to rescue personnel. Reported facial burns are the result of the friction produced when an individual strikes the air bag (similar to a rug burn).

The National Safety Council is unaware of any injuries to vehicle occupants or rescue workers because of exposure to sodium azide or other chemicals used in air bags—but is aware of thousands of deaths and injuries averted through use of air bags in conjunction with safety belts.

Emergency workers: It's unlikely that an air bag will fail to deploy during a severe frontal impact, but if this should occur, the system can be deactivated by cutting both of the car's battery cables. If the driver is pinned behind a steering wheel or instrument panel with an undeployed air bag, do not attempt to remove the victim, drill, cut or apply heat to the steering hub or the air bag module until the battery cables are cut.

Safety Belts

Safety belts can save up to 15,000 lives and prevent hundreds of thousands of serious injuries each year—but only if you wear them. (Low and snug, please.) Studies by the National Highway Traffic Safety Administration show **you're only half as likely to be critically injured—or die—in a crash if you're wearing your safety belt.**

And not just on the turnpike. Half of all serious motor vehicle injuries occur at speeds under 40 miles an hour. (For one thing, if you're hit by a drunk coming at you at an equally modest 40 mph, the two of you are going 80.) Fatalities involving nonbelted occupants have been actually recorded at speeds as low as 12 mph (probably gunshot wounds from other drivers stuck behind, trying to pass). And since 83% of all accidents occur less than 25 miles from home, safety belts are not just for the trip to Orlando—they're for the trip to the store.

Happily, safety belt use is on the rise. More than 40 states now have safety belt laws. In those, safety belts are now worn a little more than half the time. In states without laws, safety belts are worn a little more than a third of the time. But both rates are still amazingly low when you consider how many people are confined to wheelchairs for the rest of their lives, in many cases crippling their families financially in the process, just because they were too cool to buckle up.

And don't forget **kiddie seats,** for children too young to wear safety belts.

Myth: It's better to be "thrown clear" of the car in an accident.
Fact: The biggest problem with this is that you frequently have to be thrown through your car's windshield first. Furthermore, the National Safety Council deadpans, "The force of a collision could hurl you as much as fifteen car lengths. Once airborne, you would risk landing on a roadside object and being run over by another vehicle." *You're about 25 times more likely to die if ejected from your car than if inside and belted.*

Myth: Safety belts could trap me if the car catches fire or sinks.
Fact: Less than one-half of one percent of all injury-producing collisions involve fire or submersion. But even in those cases, safety belts can save lives. The unrestrained occupant will be slammed into the dashboard or windshield and knocked unconscious, unable to extricate himself. Belts keep occupants unhurt, conscious, and alert. Also, an unrestrained occupant rendered unconscious could block the exit of other occupants.

Myth: At slow speeds, I could just brace myself if I saw I was going to hit something.
Fact: If you are traveling at 20 mph and weigh 150 pounds, you will hit the dashboard with a force of 3,000 pounds. Also, one out of four serious in-vehicle injuries is caused by occupants being thrown against each other.

Myth: Good drivers don't need to wear safety belts.
Fact: Apart from the obvious—that you can be hit by a bad driver (50% of all fatal car crashes involve a drinking driver)—safety belts can make good drivers better. A belted driver will have more control over the vehicle in emergencies. Finally, even good drivers occasionally need to make sudden stops. They and their occupants are less likely to be hurt if they're wearing safety belts.

Myth: I've got automatic shoulder straps, so I don't have to worry.
Fact: If only your shoulder straps are automatic, studies show you are probably not taking the trouble to fasten your lap belt as well. This is a *big* mistake. During a crash, the shoulder belt helps keep

your head and chest from striking the steering wheel, dashboard, and windshield. The lap belt can keep you in the seat and stop your body from "submarining" under the shoulder belt.

Myth: Safety belts don't work. They hang loose or don't lock up when pulled.
Fact: Many cars are equipped with a one-piece lap-shoulder belt deliberately designed to allow freedom of movement, to make them less confining and to allow easy access to, say, the glove compartment, or to smack one of the kids. When needed, an inertial device locks these safety belts in place.

Myth: Safety belts cause injuries.
Fact: Injuries from belts have been reported. In these rare situations, however, either the belt was inappropriately worn or the crash was so severe that the occupants would almost surely have been at least as seriously injured anyway.

Appendix C:

TEAR-OUT LETTERS TO YOUR GOVERNOR

You don't need my help writing a letter. But if you're as busy as most people are these days, consider just ripping out one of the two that follow and sending it to your Governor. It should be enough to address it to him or her at "The State House" in your state's capital city.

☐ The first letter is meant to go all by itself.

☐ The second letter would be used if you're also sending a copy of this book. (The more that are received, the more likely the Governor and his staff will read at least one.)

With either letter, you might want to enclose your auto insurance policy and handwrite a PS. For example: "PS—I'm enclosing my auto insurance policy. Is anyone actually supposed to *read* this? Could anyone devise a more complicated, wasteful system than the one we have now?" As long as you keep a record of who your insurer is, and your policy number, you shouldn't need the actual policy itself.

Few things are as deadly and intimidating as insurance policies. And they carry a certain authority. A clerk who might quickly toss your letter in the trash might be less quick to can an insurance policy. If you want to be really cruel, you could ask the Governor to "Please read through it and then return it to me for safekeeping."

If you think this kind of grass-roots rabble-rousing is a little unseemly—I do, too, frankly—you could always take the more dignified route. Like the trial attorneys and others who will oppose PPN, you could just contribute a few thousand dollars to the Governor's campaign each year and have breakfast with him to cordially but firmly express your professional opinion.

Dear Governor:

Why do we sell auto insurance one policy at a time when state law requires everyone to have it? And why does so much of our auto insurance money go to lawyers instead of accident victims?

I've just read AUTO INSURANCE ALERT!, which proposes **Pay-at-the-Pump, Private, No-Fault** auto insurance (PPN).

There'd be no sales costs, because everyone would be covered automatically. The premium would be added to the price of gas (with surcharges at registration for high-risk vehicles, and on traffic tickets so unsafe drivers pay more).

There'd be no need for a new government bureaucracy, because PPN would be *private*. Insurers would bid for the right to cover large groups of drivers just as they now compete to provide group health plans.

There'd be virtually no legal costs, because it would be TRUE no-fault.

PPN would cut costs further by eliminating duplicate reimbursements; by eliminating incentives to fraudulently "build" claims; and by limiting pain-and-suffering payments to a modest, pre-set schedule. (Anyone seeking more could buy it privately.) PPN would cover all unreimbursed medical expenses, liability, lost wages and most basic auto-repair – a lot more coverage than most of us have now.

And by collecting the premiums efficiently, at the pump instead of through the mail, we would totally eliminate the problem of uninsured motorists – as well as powerfully encourage energy conservation (with all the attendant benefits of that).

You've probably already read AUTO INSURANCE ALERT! If you haven't, I hope you'll somehow find time to do so. This is no more pie-in-the-sky than, say, "group health insurance" or "workers' comp" – concepts I assume you support. In fact, in some ways it's better, because it starts with a fresh slate.

Thank you very much for taking the time to look into this.

Sincerely,

Dear Governor:

You've probably already read AUTO INSURANCE ALERT!, but I've enclosed a copy just in case. The system it proposes, called PPN (Pay-at-the-Pump, Private, No-Fault), is no more pie-in-the-sky than, say, "group health insurance" or "workers' comp" — concepts I assume you support. In fact, in some ways it's better, because it starts with a fresh slate.

Under PPN, there'd be no sales costs, because everyone would be covered automatically. The premium would be added to the price of gas (with surcharges at registration for high-risk vehicles, and on traffic tickets so unsafe drivers pay more).

There'd be no need for a new government bureaucracy, because PPN would be *private*. Insurers would bid for the right to cover large groups of drivers just as they now compete to provide group health plans.

There'd be virtually no legal costs, because it would be TRUE no-fault.

PPN would cut costs further by eliminating duplicate reimbursements; by eliminating incentives to fraudulently "build" claims; and by limiting pain-and-suffering payments to a modest, pre-set schedule. (Anyone seeking more could buy it privately.) PPN would cover all unreimbursed medical expenses, liability, lost wages and most basic auto-repair — a lot more coverage than most of us have now.

And by collecting the premiums efficiently, at the pump instead of through the mail, we would totally eliminate the problem of uninsured motorists — as well as powerfully encourage energy conservation (with all the attendant benefits of that).

Thank you very much for taking the time to look into this.

Sincerely,

Sign Me Up!

✄ -

I like this plan! Here's how to reach me if anything ever gets going in my state:

_____

✎ **Name**

_____

✎ **Street Address**

_____

✎ **City**   **State**   **Zip**

○ I'd sign a petition for PPN

○ I could help sign up others

✉ **Mail to: NICO, 121 N. Payne St., Alexandria, VA 22314**

About the Author

Andrew Tobias is a graduate of Harvard College and Harvard Business School. His books include *The Only Investment Guide You'll Ever Need* ("The only investment guide many will indeed ever need," said *Barrons*) and its companion, *The Only OTHER Investment Guide You'll Ever Need* (oops) . . . as well as *Fire and Ice, Money Angles,* and *The Invisible Bankers* ("Tobias is a balanced writer with a strong appreciation of insurance's basic virtues," wrote *Fortune*). His computer software, *Managing Your Money,* has been a best-seller since 1984. A columnist for *Time,* Tobias has appeared on such television shows as Today, Tonight, Tomorrow, and the MacNeil-Lehrer Hour.